BLOOD UPON THE ROSE
EASTER 1916
THE REBELLION THAT SET IRELAND FREE

WRITTEN AND DRAWN BY
GERRY HUNT

COLOURED BY
BRENB

THE O'BRIEN PRESS
DUBLIN

To my father, Patrick Hunt, who was active in the 1916 Rising and the War of Independence.
G.H.

To my grandparents, Bridie, John, Josephine and James.
B.

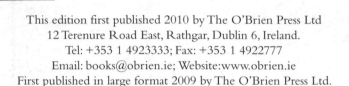

This edition first published 2010 by The O'Brien Press Ltd
12 Terenure Road East, Rathgar, Dublin 6, Ireland.
Tel: +353 1 4923333; Fax: +353 1 4922777
Email: books@obrien.ie; Website:www.obrien.ie
First published in large format 2009 by The O'Brien Press Ltd.

ISBN: 978-1-84717-217-4

The O'Brien Press receives assistance from

the arts council
an chomhairle ealaíon

British Library Cataloguing-in-Publication Data
A catalogue record for this title is available from The British Library

2 3 4 5 6 7 8 9
10 11 12 13 14

Printing: Graphy CEMS

Wednesday 3rd May 1916

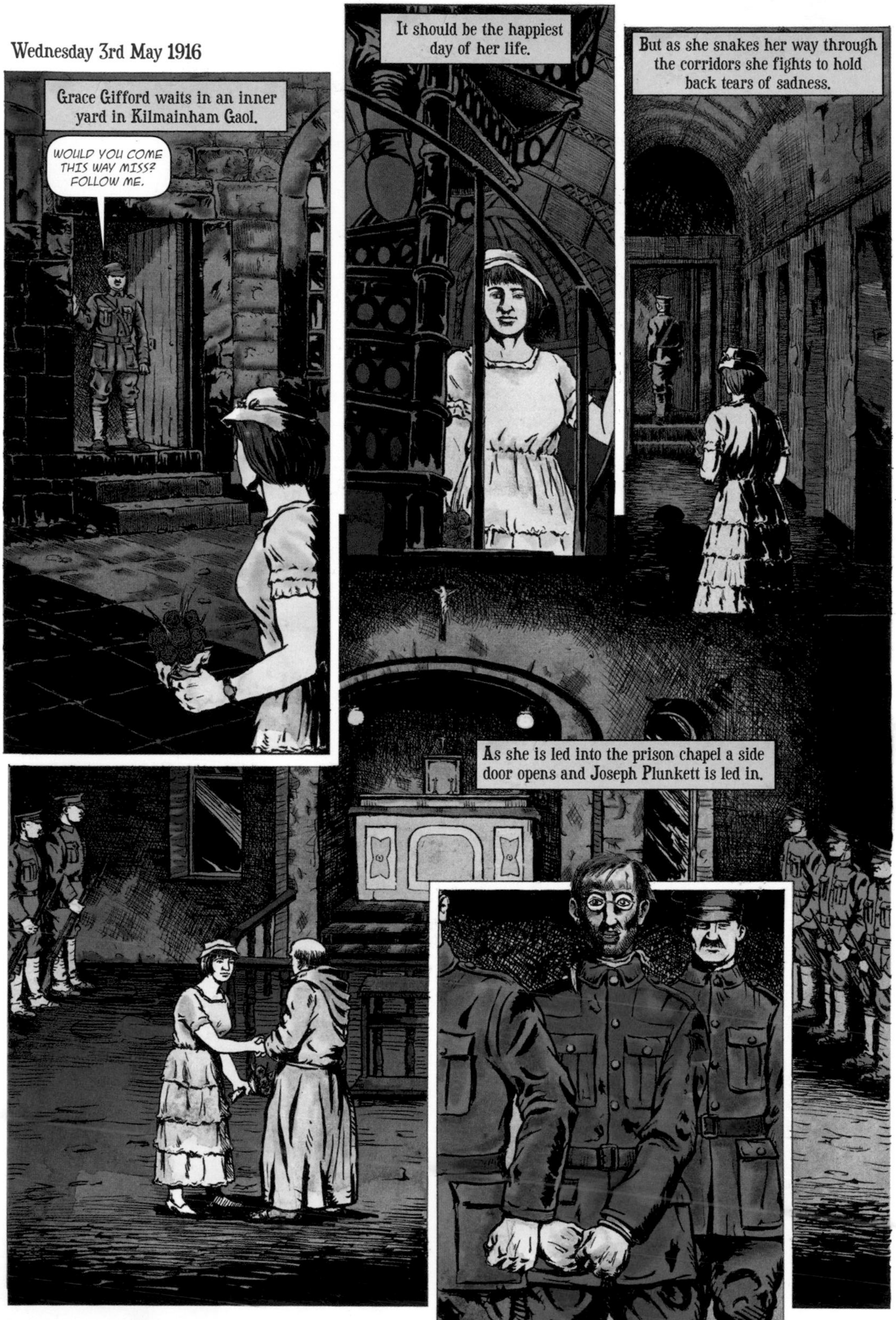
Grace Gifford waits in an inner yard in Kilmainham Gaol.
WOULD YOU COME THIS WAY MISS? FOLLOW ME.
It should be the happiest day of her life.
But as she snakes her way through the corridors she fights to hold back tears of sadness.
As she is led into the prison chapel a side door opens and Joseph Plunkett is led in.

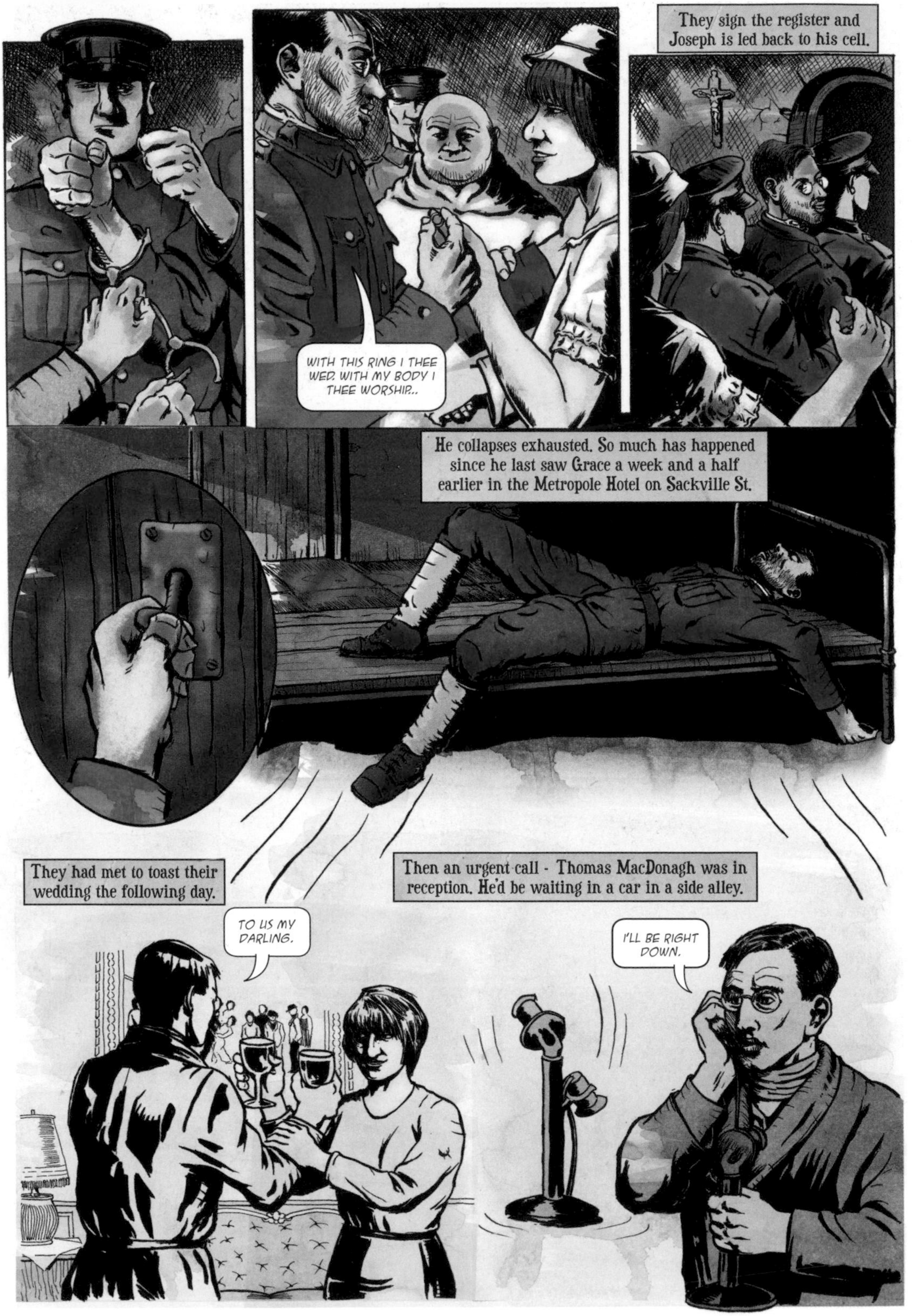
WITH THIS RING I THEE WED. WITH MY BODY I THEE WORSHIP...
They sign the register and Joseph is led back to his cell.
He collapses exhausted. So much has happened since he last saw Grace a week and a half earlier in the Metropole Hotel on Sackville St.
They had met to toast their wedding the following day.
TO US MY DARLING.
Then an urgent call - Thomas MacDonagh was in reception. He'd be waiting in a car in a side alley.
I'LL BE RIGHT DOWN.

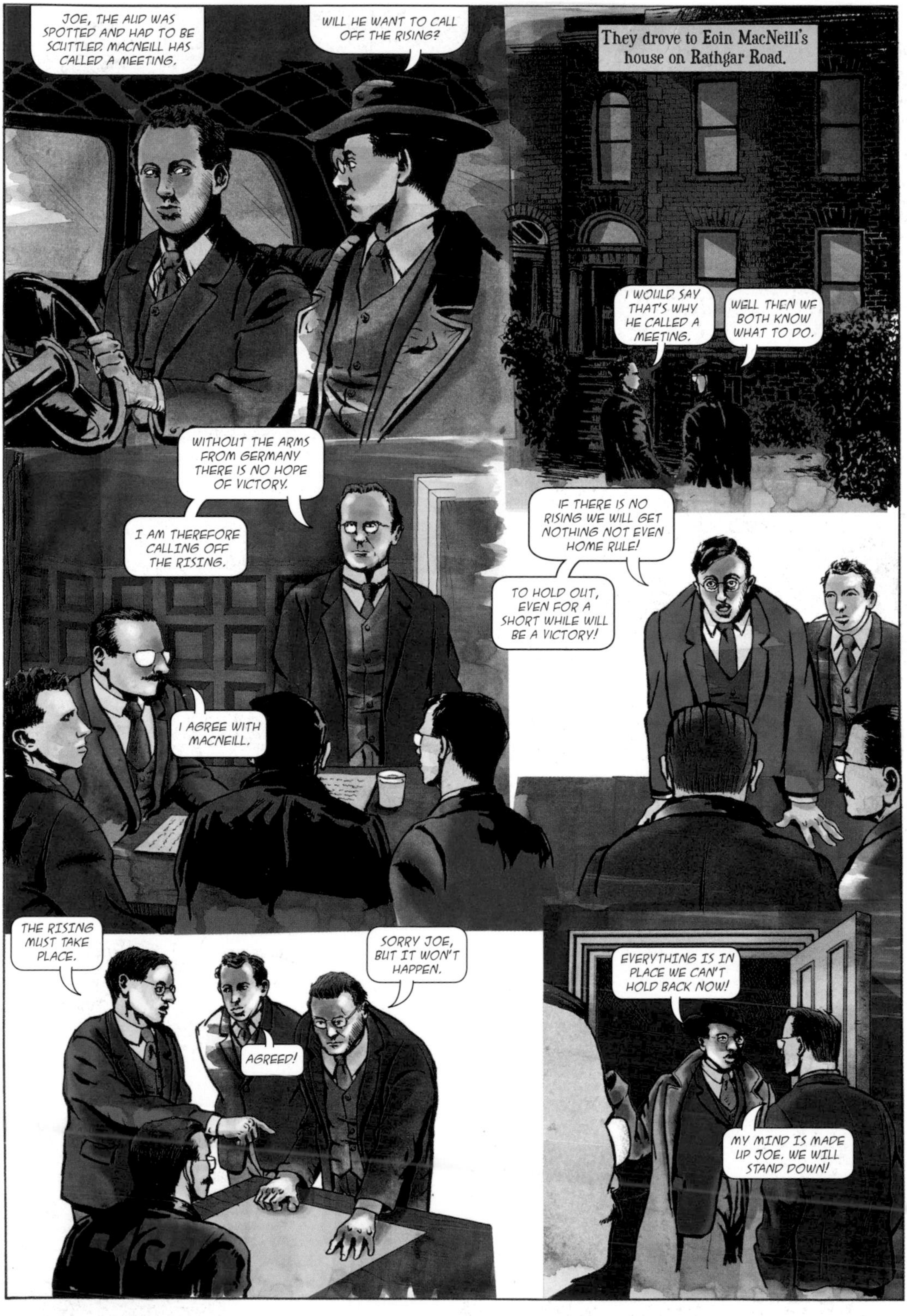
JOE, THE AUD WAS SPOTTED AND HAD TO BE SCUTTLED. MACNEILL HAS CALLED A MEETING.
WILL HE WANT TO CALL OFF THE RISING?
They drove to Eoin MacNeill's house on Rathgar Road.
I WOULD SAY THAT'S WHY HE CALLED A MEETING.
WELL THEN WE BOTH KNOW WHAT TO DO.
WITHOUT THE ARMS FROM GERMANY THERE IS NO HOPE OF VICTORY.
I AM THEREFORE CALLING OFF THE RISING.
I AGREE WITH MACNEILL.
IF THERE IS NO RISING WE WILL GET NOTHING NOT EVEN HOME RULE!
TO HOLD OUT, EVEN FOR A SHORT WHILE WILL BE A VICTORY!
THE RISING MUST TAKE PLACE.
SORRY JOE, BUT IT WON'T HAPPEN.
AGREED!
EVERYTHING IS IN PLACE WE CAN'T HOLD BACK NOW!
MY MIND IS MADE UP JOE. WE WILL STAND DOWN!

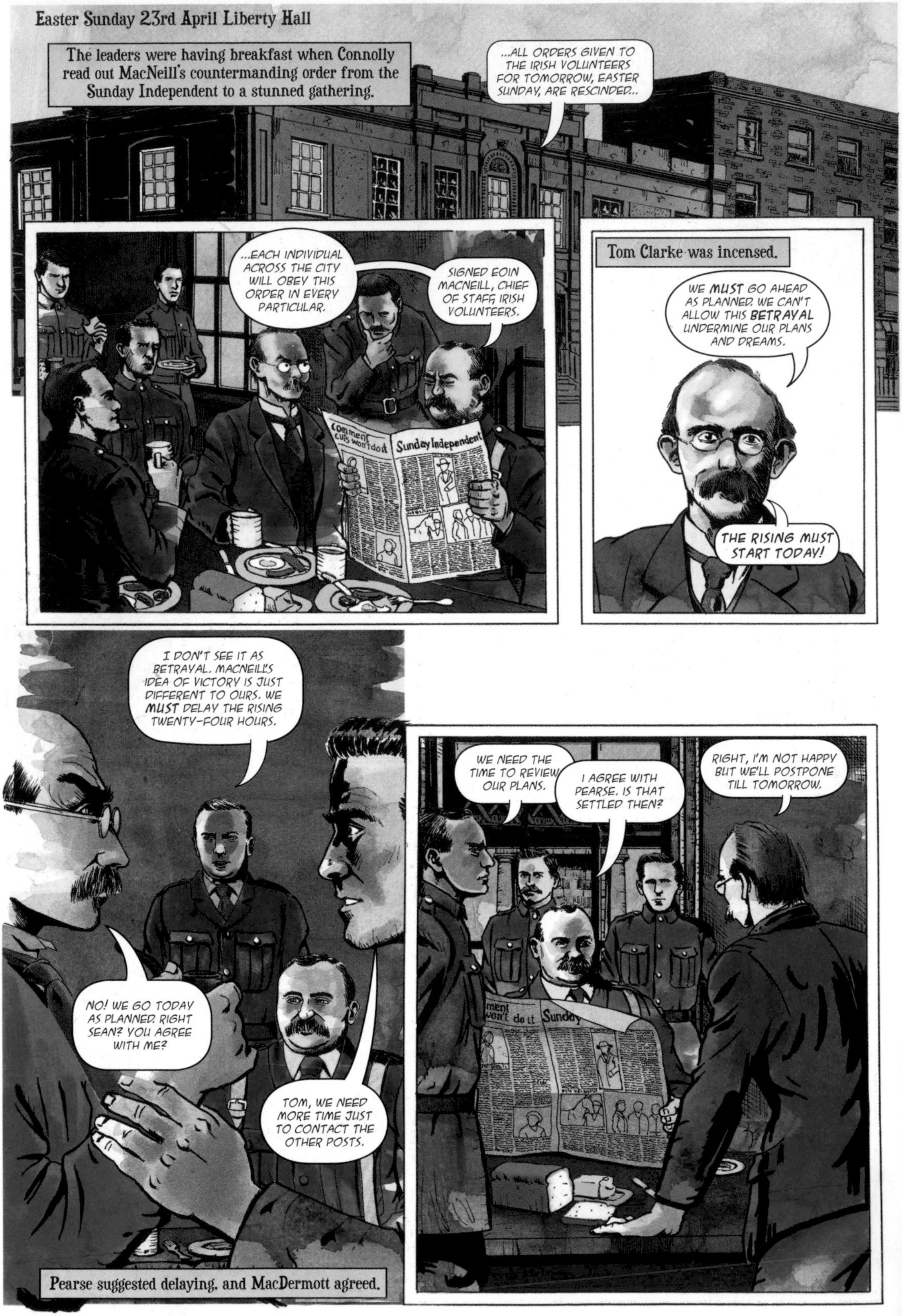
Easter Sunday 23rd April Liberty Hall
The leaders were having breakfast when Connolly read out MacNeill's countermanding order from the Sunday Independent to a stunned gathering.
...ALL ORDERS GIVEN TO THE IRISH VOLUNTEERS FOR TOMORROW, EASTER SUNDAY, ARE RESCINDED...
...EACH INDIVIDUAL ACROSS THE CITY WILL OBEY THIS ORDER IN EVERY PARTICULAR.
SIGNED EOIN MACNEILL, CHIEF OF STAFF, IRISH VOLUNTEERS.
Sunday Independent
Tom Clarke was incensed.
WE MUST GO AHEAD AS PLANNED. WE CAN'T ALLOW THIS BETRAYAL UNDERMINE OUR PLANS AND DREAMS.
THE RISING MUST START TODAY!
I DON'T SEE IT AS BETRAYAL. MACNEILL'S IDEA OF VICTORY IS JUST DIFFERENT TO OURS. WE MUST DELAY THE RISING TWENTY-FOUR HOURS.
NO! WE GO TODAY AS PLANNED. RIGHT SEAN? YOU AGREE WITH ME?
TOM, WE NEED MORE TIME JUST TO CONTACT THE OTHER POSTS.
Pearse suggested delaying, and MacDermott agreed.
WE NEED THE TIME TO REVIEW OUR PLANS.
I AGREE WITH PEARSE. IS THAT SETTLED THEN?
RIGHT, I'M NOT HAPPY BUT WE'LL POSTPONE TILL TOMORROW.

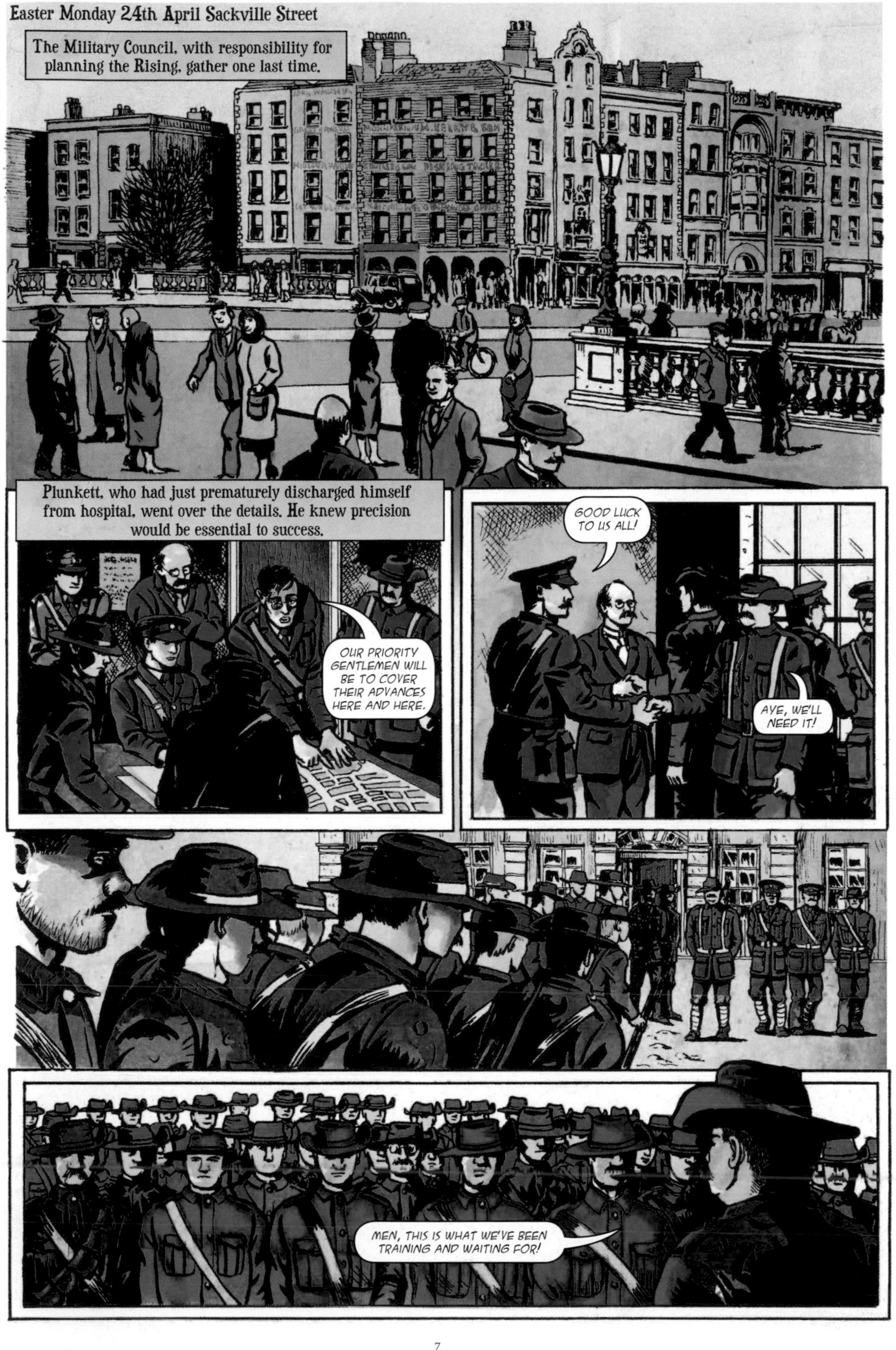
Easter Monday 24th April Sackville Street
The Military Council, with responsibility for planning the Rising, gather one last time.
Plunkett, who had just prematurely discharged himself from hospital, went over the details. He knew precision would be essential to success.
OUR PRIORITY GENTLEMEN WILL BE TO COVER THEIR ADVANCES HERE AND HERE.
GOOD LUCK TO US ALL!
AYE, WE'LL NEED IT!
MEN, THIS IS WHAT WE'VE BEEN TRAINING AND WAITING FOR!

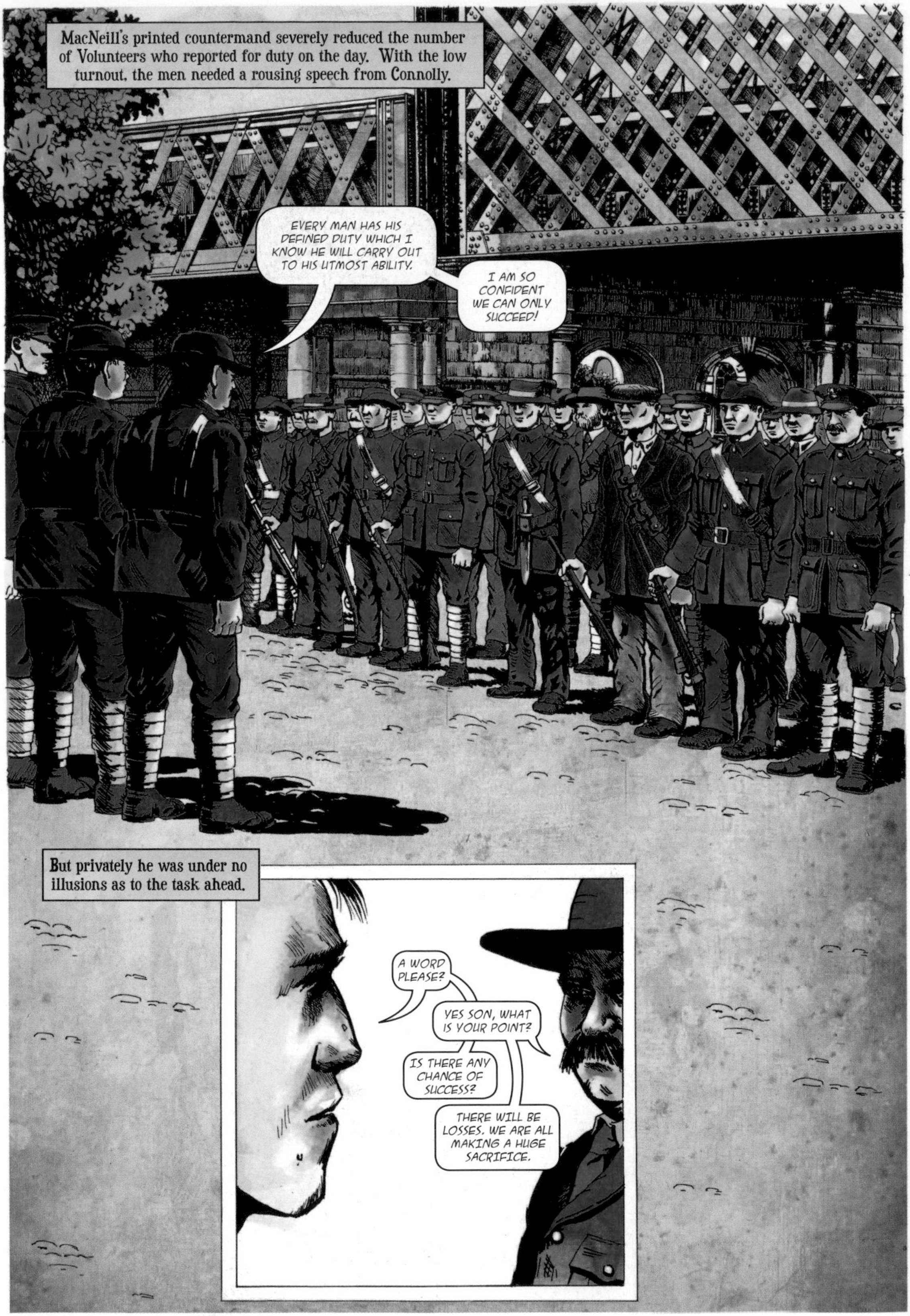
MacNeill's printed countermand severely reduced the number of Volunteers who reported for duty on the day. With the low turnout, the men needed a rousing speech from Connolly.
EVERY MAN HAS HIS DEFINED DUTY WHICH I KNOW HE WILL CARRY OUT TO HIS UTMOST ABILITY.
I AM SO CONFIDENT WE CAN ONLY SUCCEED!
But privately he was under no illusions as to the task ahead.
A WORD PLEASE?
YES SON, WHAT IS YOUR POINT?
IS THERE ANY CHANCE OF SUCCESS?
THERE WILL BE LOSSES. WE ARE ALL MAKING A HUGE SACRIFICE.

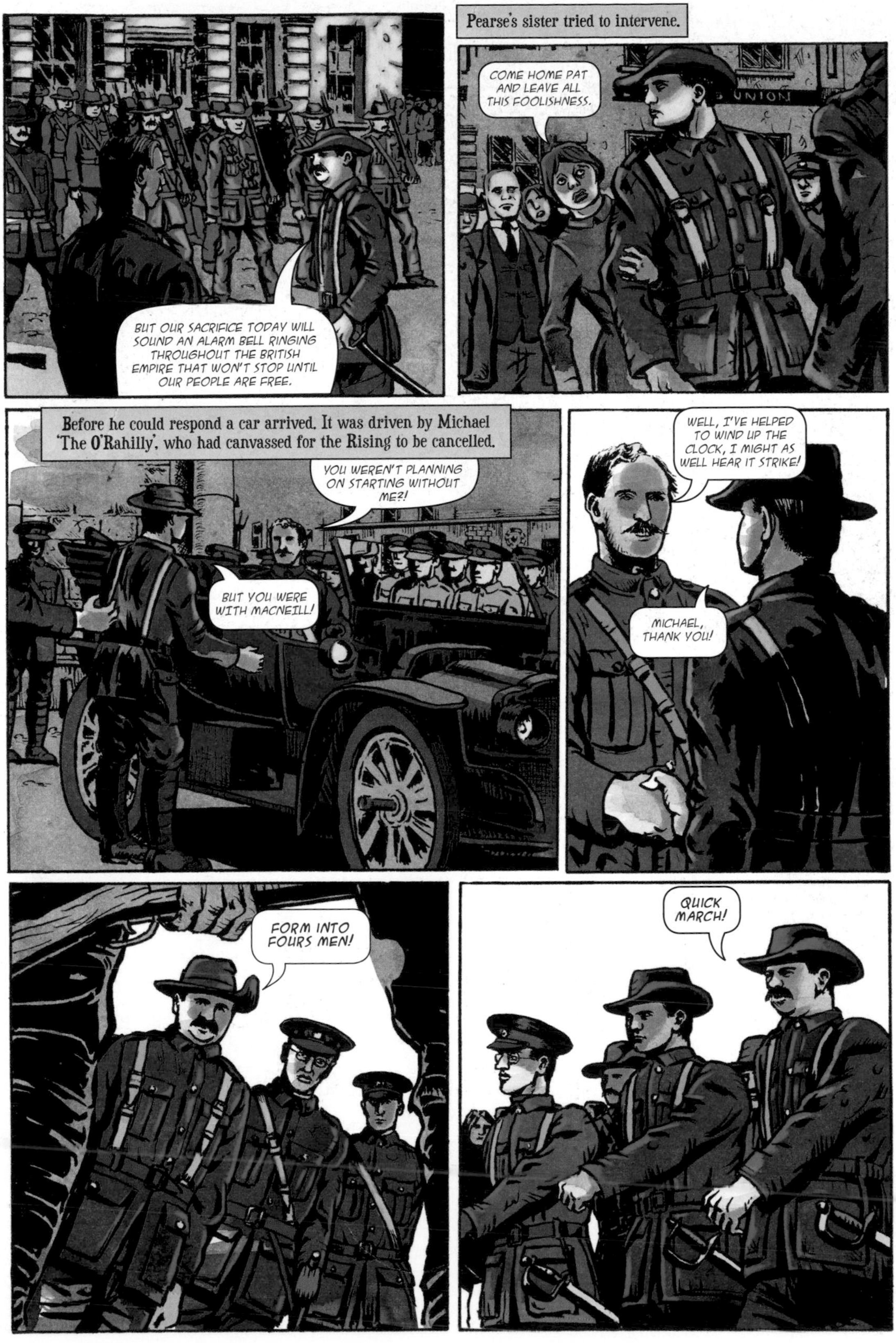
BUT OUR SACRIFICE TODAY WILL SOUND AN ALARM BELL RINGING THROUGHOUT THE BRITISH EMPIRE THAT WON'T STOP UNTIL OUR PEOPLE ARE FREE.
Pearse's sister tried to intervene.
COME HOME PAT AND LEAVE ALL THIS FOOLISHNESS.
Before he could respond a car arrived. It was driven by Michael 'The O'Rahilly', who had canvassed for the Rising to be cancelled.
YOU WEREN'T PLANNING ON STARTING WITHOUT ME?!
BUT YOU WERE WITH MACNEILL!
WELL, I'VE HELPED TO WIND UP THE CLOCK, I MIGHT AS WELL HEAR IT STRIKE!
MICHAEL, THANK YOU!
FORM INTO FOURS MEN!
QUICK MARCH!

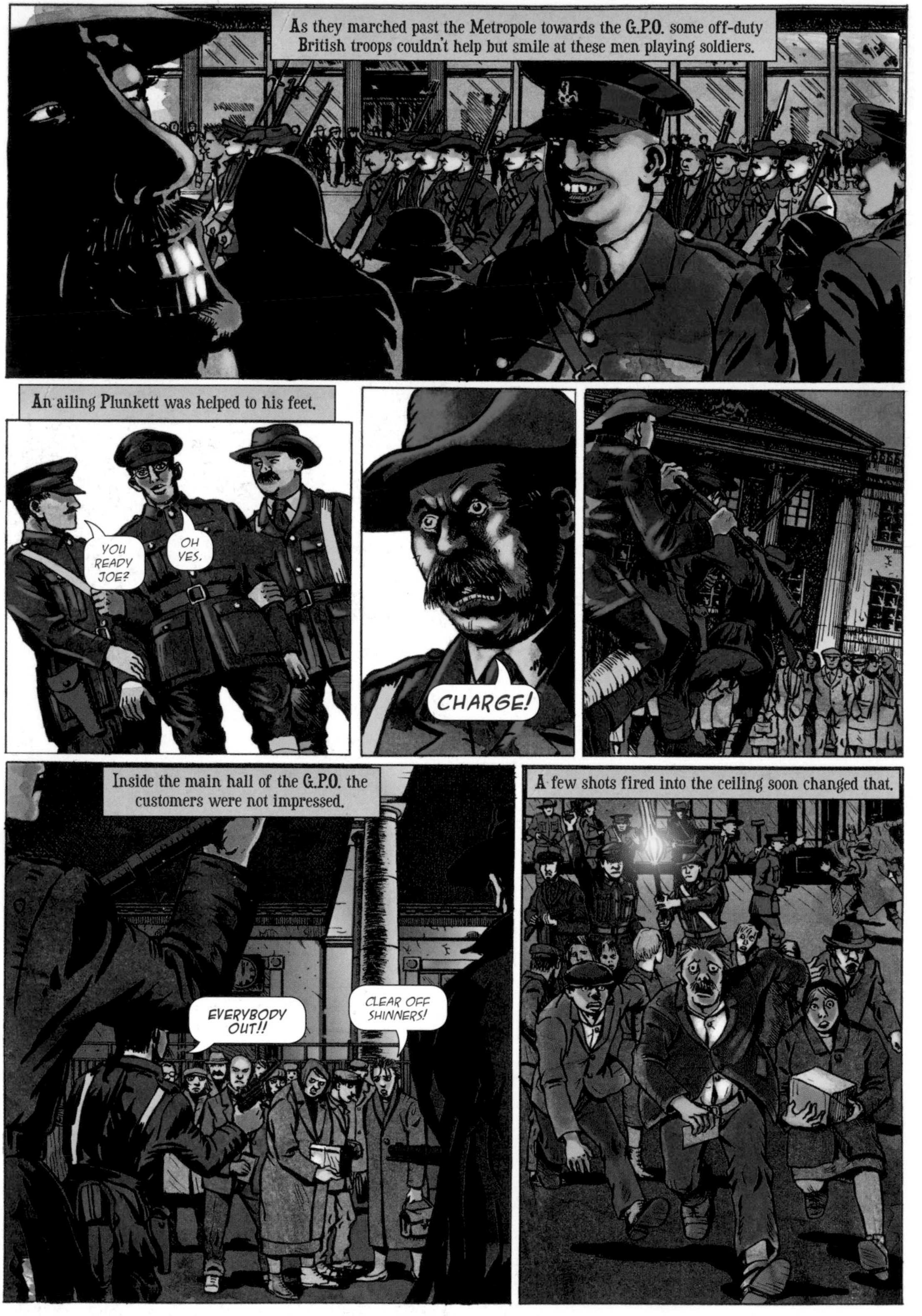
As they marched past the Metropole towards the G.P.O. some off-duty British troops couldn't help but smile at these men playing soldiers.
An ailing Plunkett was helped to his feet.
YOU READY JOE?
OH YES.
CHARGE!
Inside the main hall of the G.P.O. the customers were not impressed.
EVERYBODY OUT!!
CLEAR OFF SHINNERS!
A few shots fired into the ceiling soon changed that.

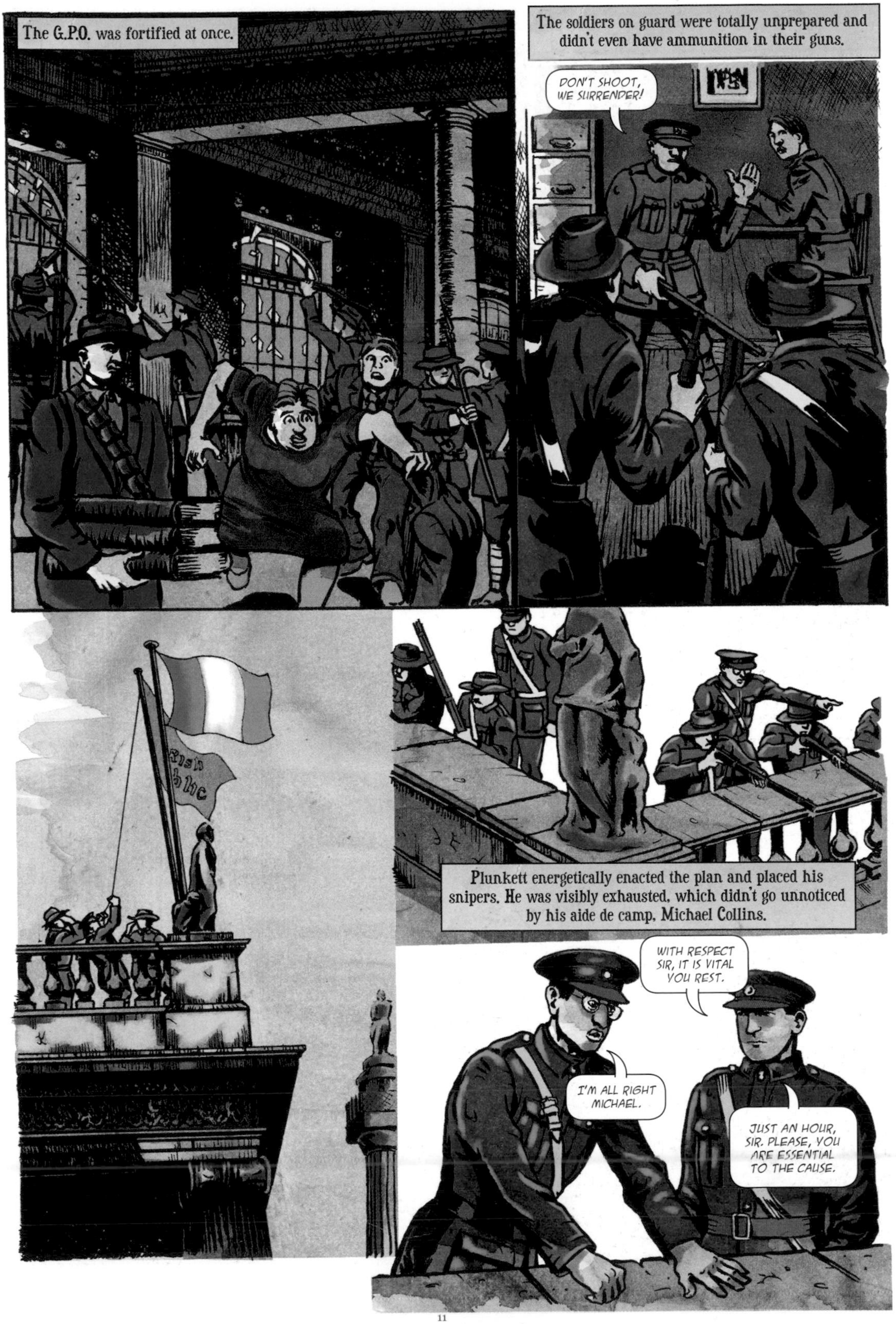
The G.P.O. was fortified at once.
The soldiers on guard were totally unprepared and didn't even have ammunition in their guns.
DON'T SHOOT, WE SURRENDER!
Plunkett energetically enacted the plan and placed his snipers. He was visibly exhausted, which didn't go unnoticed by his aide de camp, Michael Collins.
WITH RESPECT SIR, IT IS VITAL YOU REST.
I'M ALL RIGHT MICHAEL.
JUST AN HOUR, SIR. PLEASE, YOU ARE ESSENTIAL TO THE CAUSE.

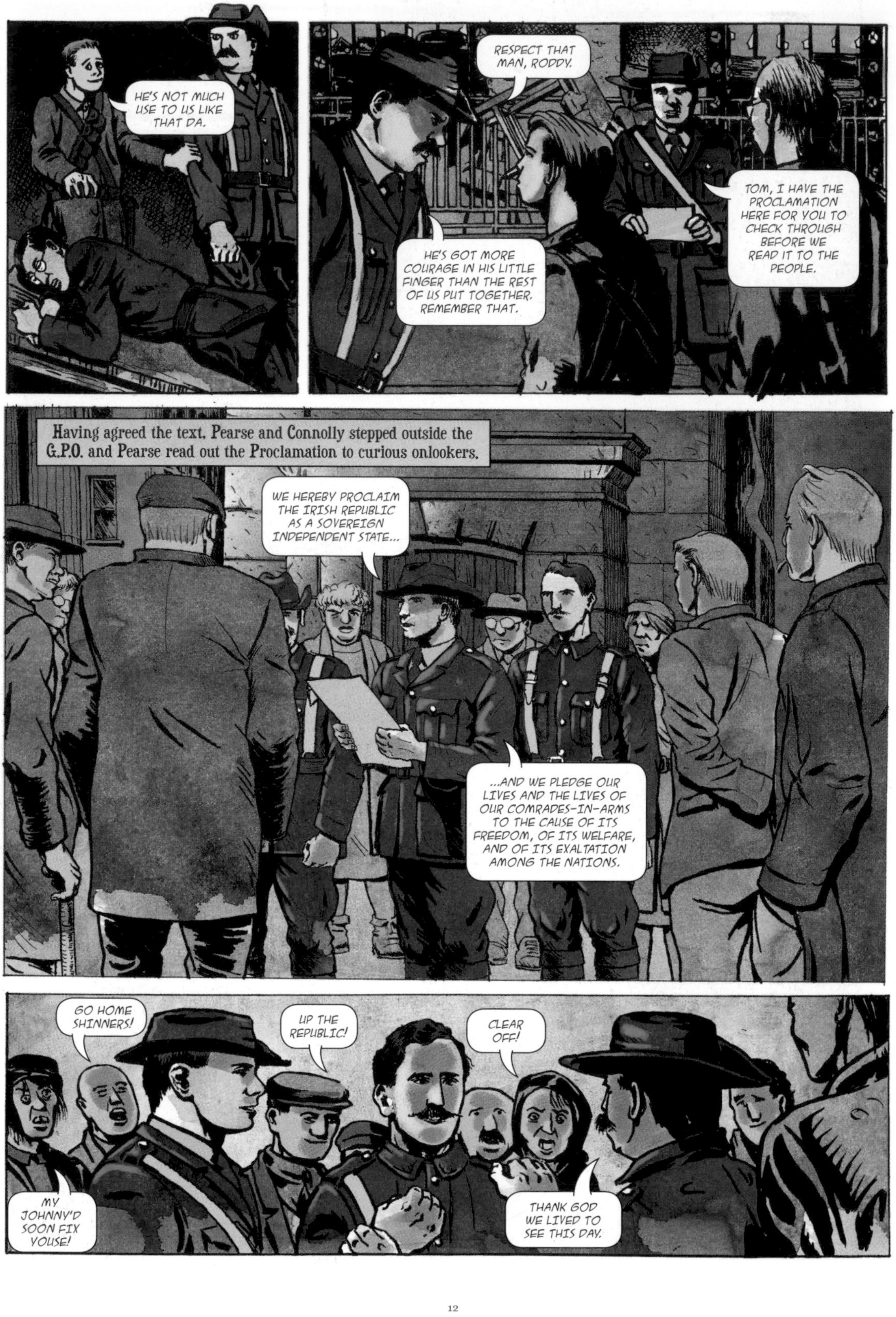
HE'S NOT MUCH USE TO US LIKE THAT DA.
RESPECT THAT MAN, RODDY.
HE'S GOT MORE COURAGE IN HIS LITTLE FINGER THAN THE REST OF US PUT TOGETHER. REMEMBER THAT.
TOM, I HAVE THE PROCLAMATION HERE FOR YOU TO CHECK THROUGH BEFORE WE READ IT TO THE PEOPLE.
Having agreed the text, Pearse and Connolly stepped outside the G.P.O. and Pearse read out the Proclamation to curious onlookers.
WE HEREBY PROCLAIM THE IRISH REPUBLIC AS A SOVEREIGN INDEPENDENT STATE...
...AND WE PLEDGE OUR LIVES AND THE LIVES OF OUR COMRADES-IN-ARMS TO THE CAUSE OF ITS FREEDOM, OF ITS WELFARE, AND OF ITS EXALTATION AMONG THE NATIONS.
GO HOME SHINNERS!
MY JOHNNY'D SOON FIX YOUSE!
UP THE REPUBLIC!
CLEAR OFF!
THANK GOD WE LIVED TO SEE THIS DAY.

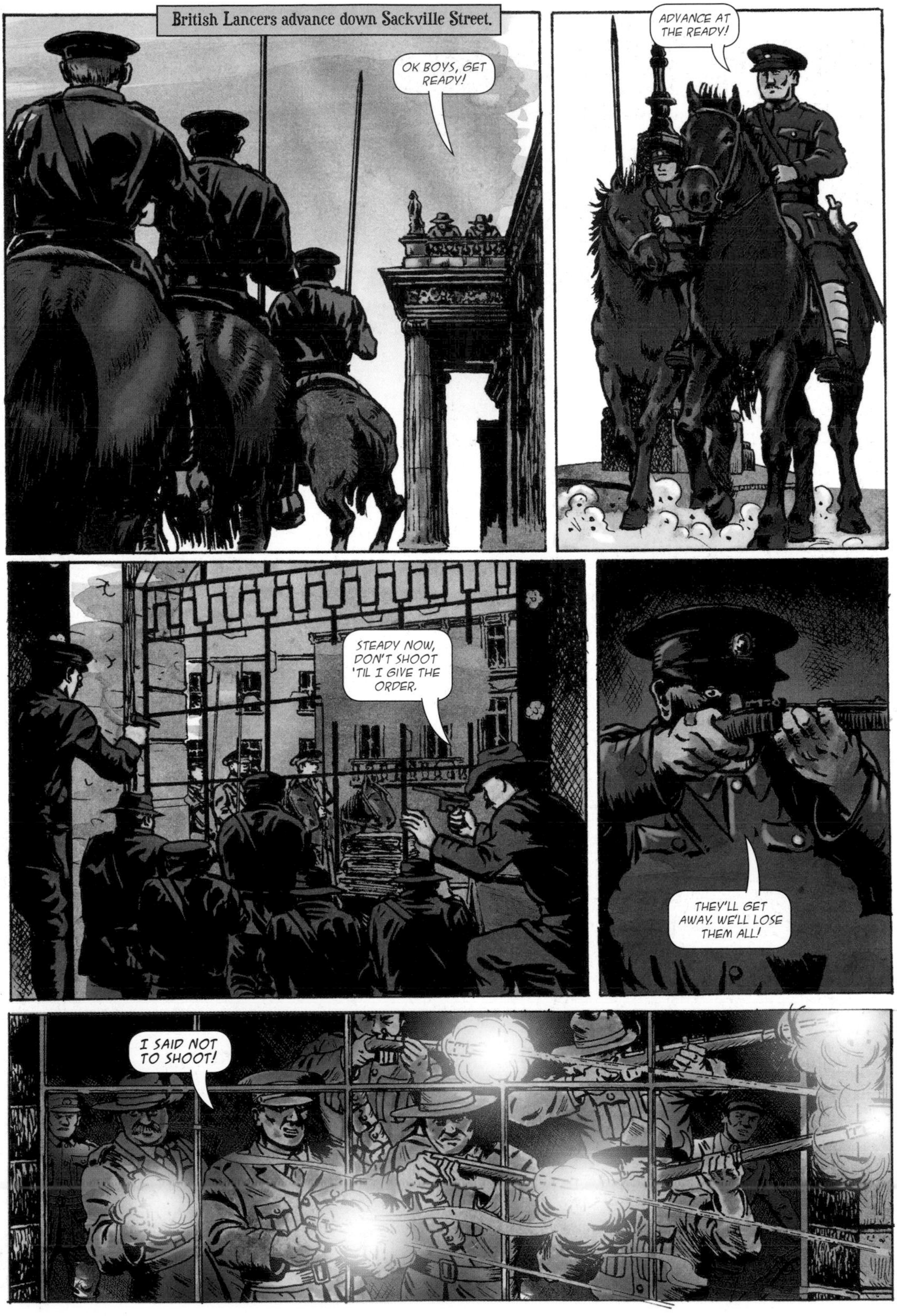
British Lancers advance down Sackville Street.
OK BOYS, GET READY!
ADVANCE AT THE READY!
STEADY NOW, DON'T SHOOT 'TIL I GIVE THE ORDER.
THEY'LL GET AWAY. WE'LL LOSE THEM ALL!
I SAID NOT TO SHOOT!

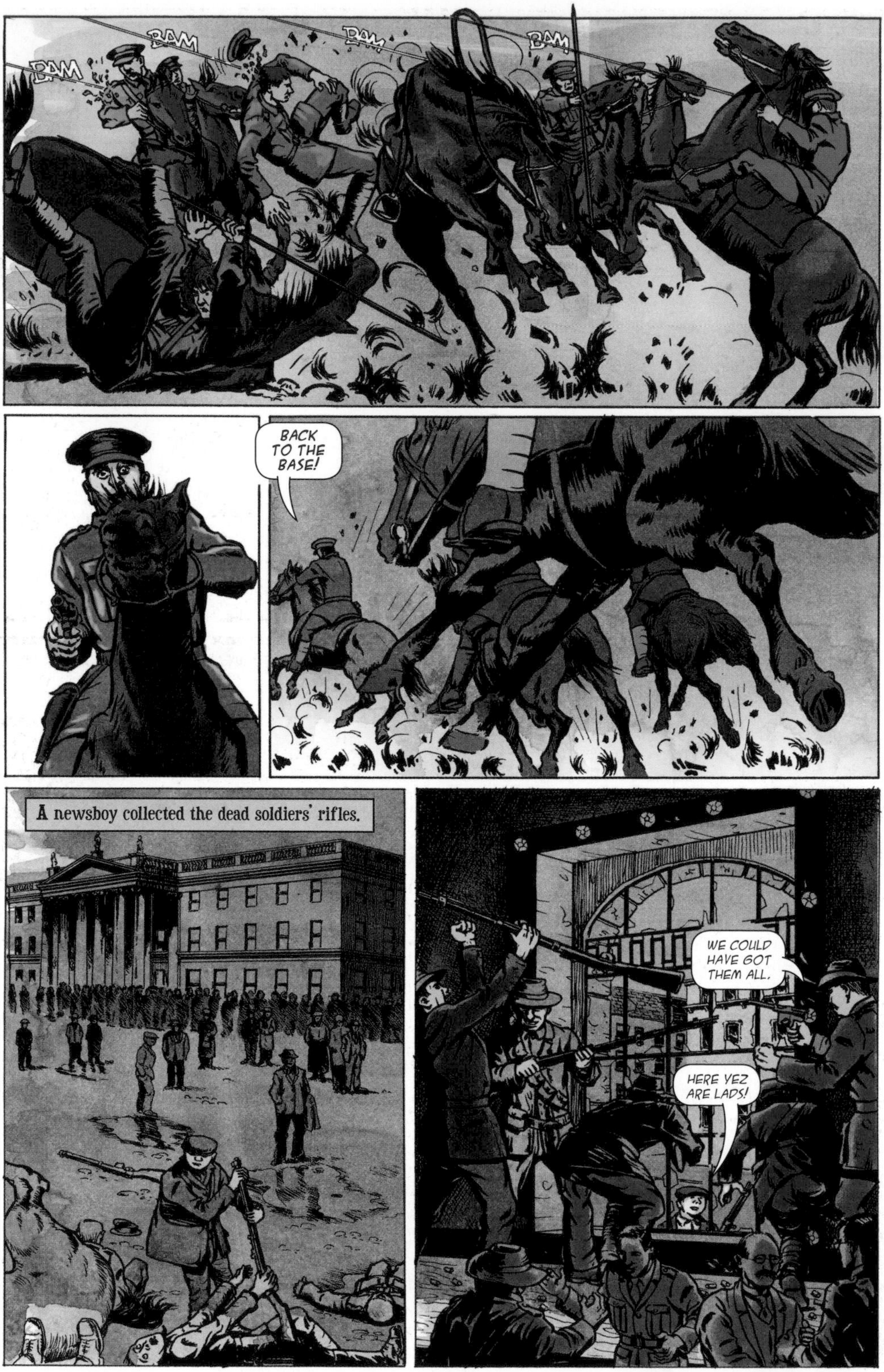
BAM
BAM
BAM
BAM
BACK TO THE BASE!
A newsboy collected the dead soldiers' rifles.
WE COULD HAVE GOT THEM ALL.
HERE YEZ ARE LADS!

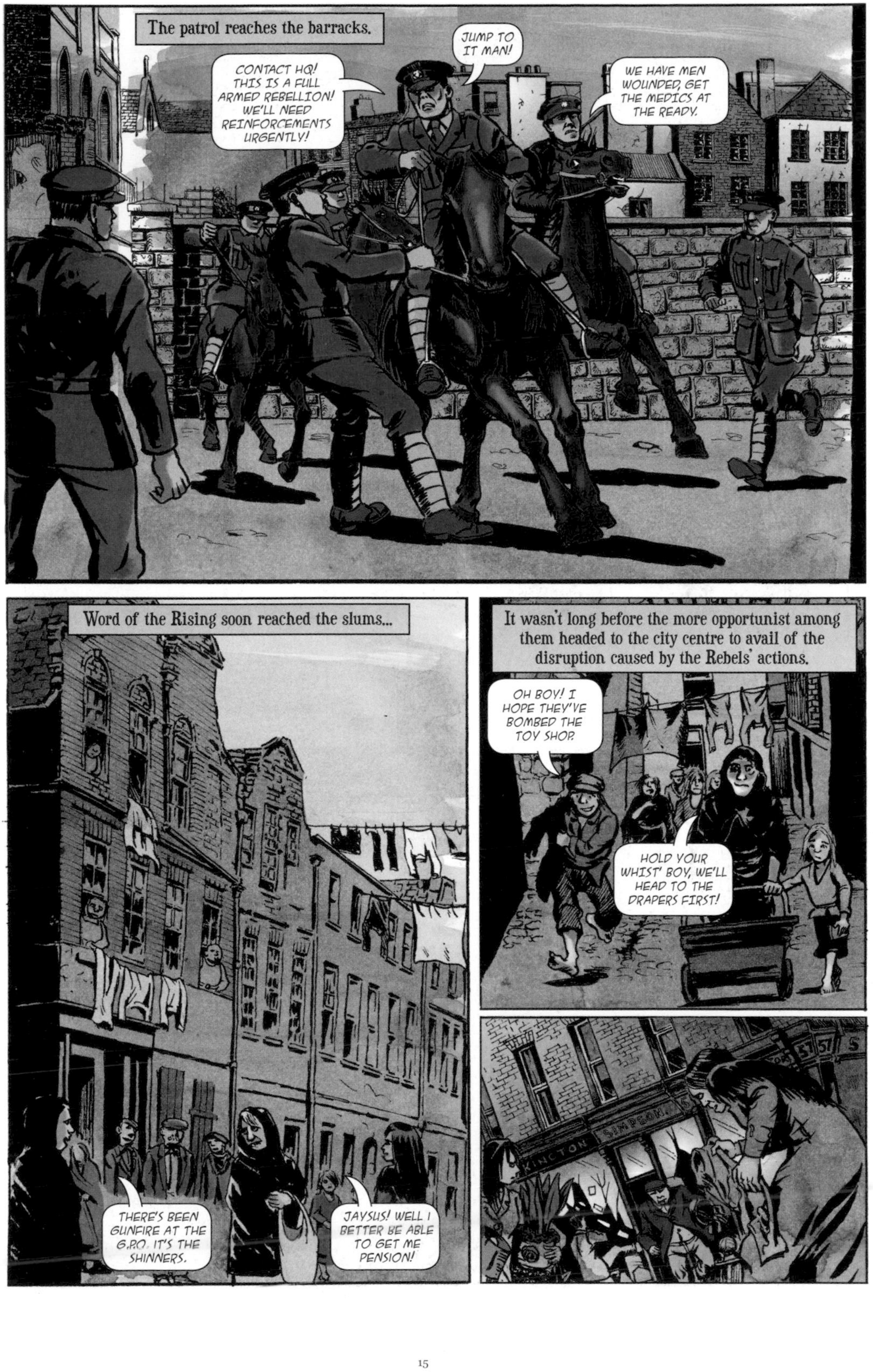
The patrol reaches the barracks.
CONTACT HQ! THIS IS A FULL ARMED REBELLION! WE'LL NEED REINFORCEMENTS URGENTLY!
JUMP TO IT MAN!
WE HAVE MEN WOUNDED, GET THE MEDICS AT THE READY.
Word of the Rising soon reached the slums...
THERE'S BEEN GUNFIRE AT THE G.P.O. IT'S THE SHINNERS.
JAYSUS! WELL I BETTER BE ABLE TO GET ME PENSION!
It wasn't long before the more opportunist among them headed to the city centre to avail of the disruption caused by the Rebels' actions.
OH BOY! I HOPE THEY'VE BOMBED THE TOY SHOP.
HOLD YOUR WHIST' BOY, WE'LL HEAD TO THE DRAPERS FIRST!
SIMPSON

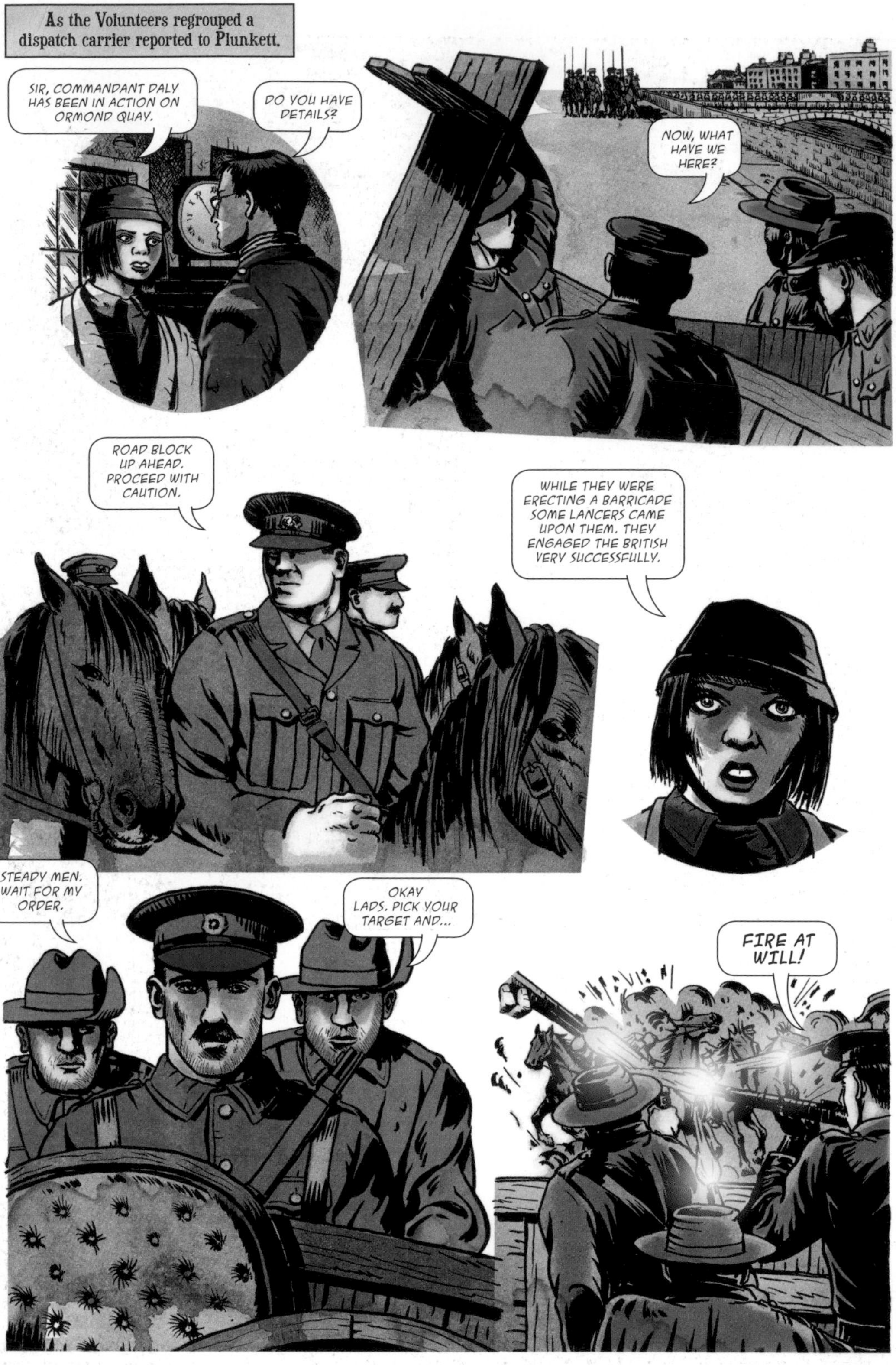
As the Volunteers regrouped a dispatch carrier reported to Plunkett.
SIR, COMMANDANT DALY HAS BEEN IN ACTION ON ORMOND QUAY.
DO YOU HAVE DETAILS?
NOW, WHAT HAVE WE HERE?
ROAD BLOCK UP AHEAD. PROCEED WITH CAUTION.
WHILE THEY WERE ERECTING A BARRICADE SOME LANCERS CAME UPON THEM. THEY ENGAGED THE BRITISH VERY SUCCESSFULLY.
STEADY MEN. WAIT FOR MY ORDER.
OKAY LADS. PICK YOUR TARGET AND...
FIRE AT WILL!

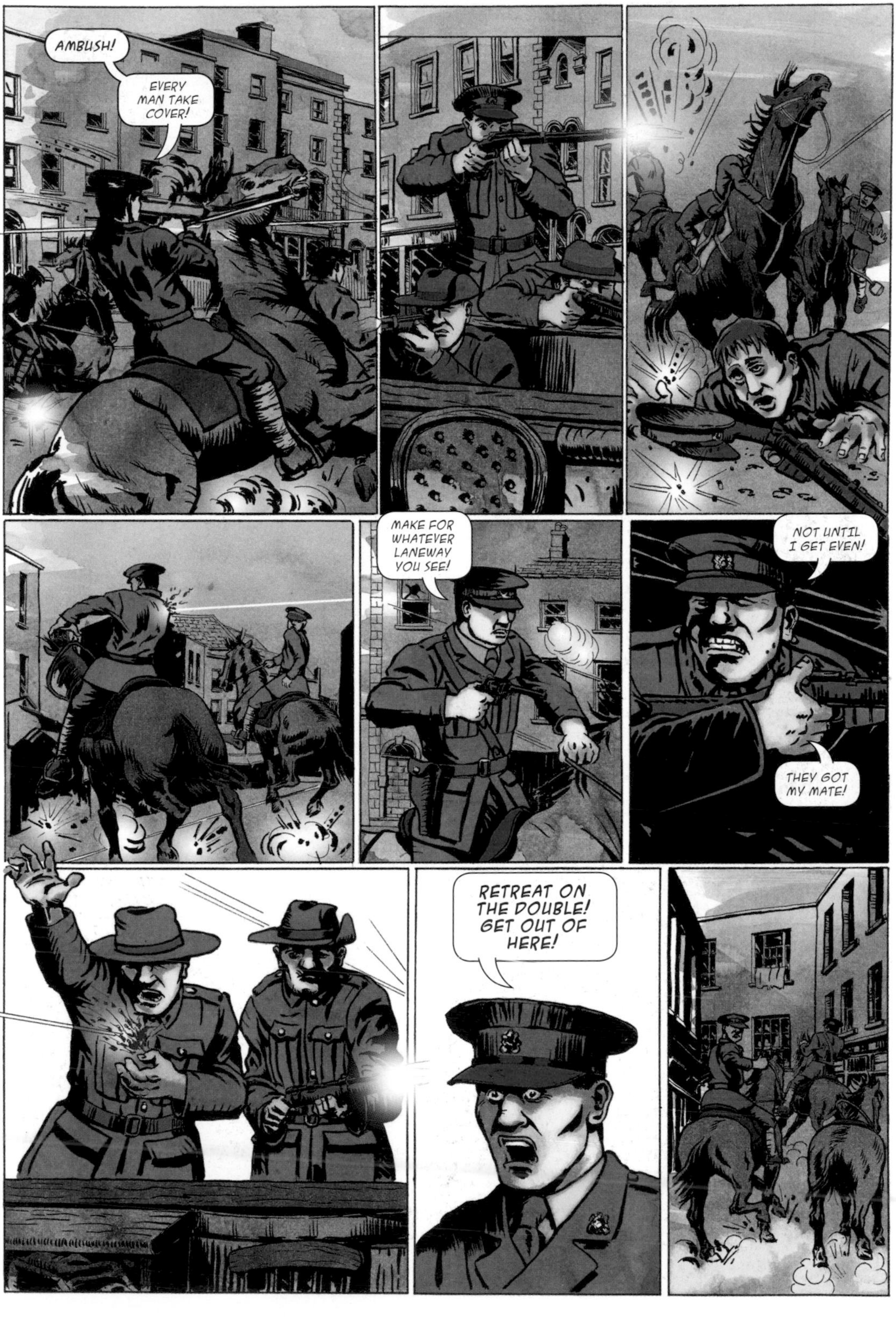
AMBUSH!
EVERY MAN TAKE COVER!
MAKE FOR WHATEVER LANEWAY YOU SEE!
NOT UNTIL I GET EVEN!
THEY GOT MY MATE!
RETREAT ON THE DOUBLE! GET OUT OF HERE!

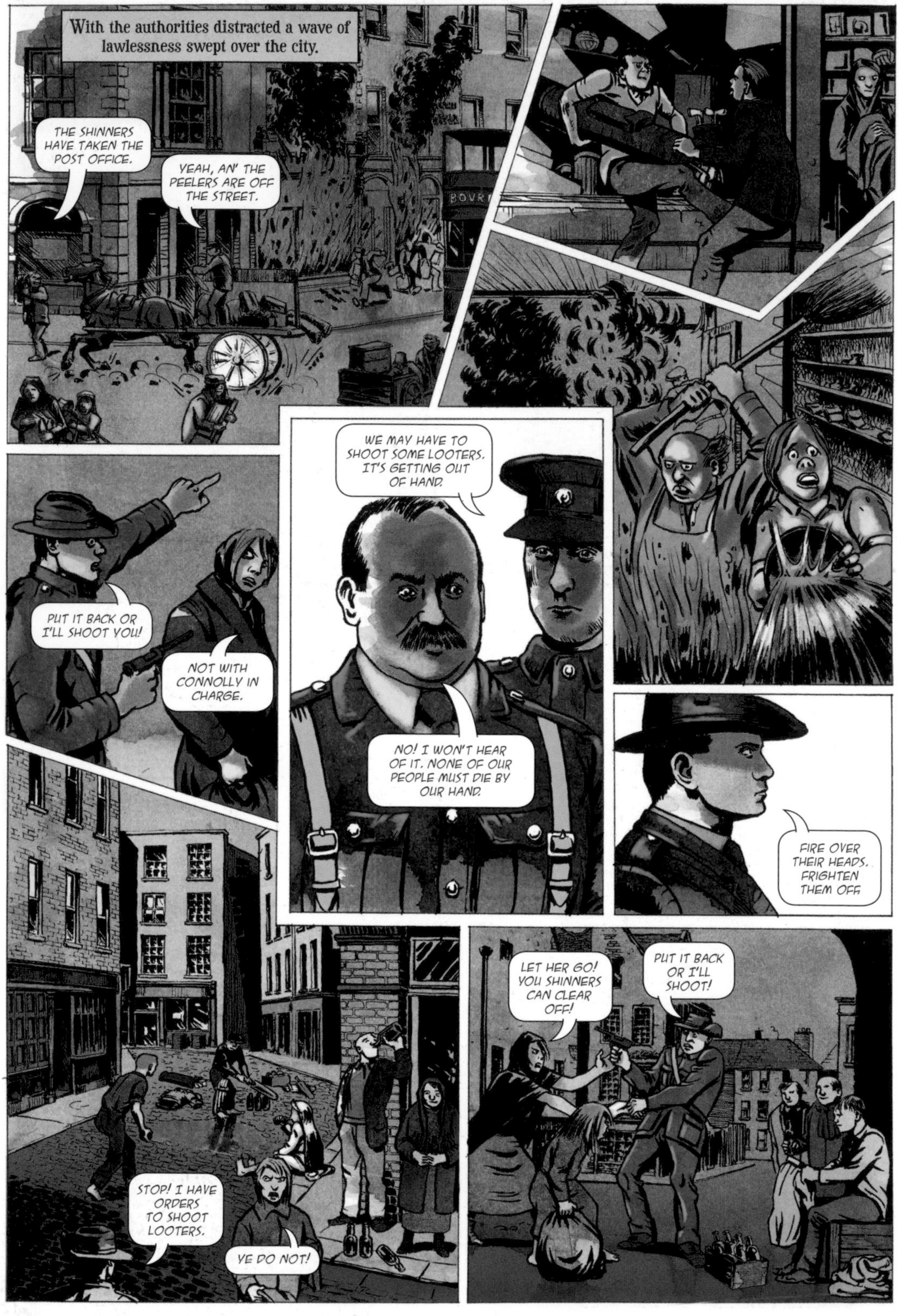
With the authorities distracted a wave of lawlessness swept over the city.
THE SHINNERS HAVE TAKEN THE POST OFFICE.
YEAH, AN' THE PEELERS ARE OFF THE STREET.
BOVRI
WE MAY HAVE TO SHOOT SOME LOOTERS. IT'S GETTING OUT OF HAND.
PUT IT BACK OR I'LL SHOOT YOU!
NOT WITH CONNOLLY IN CHARGE.
NO! I WON'T HEAR OF IT. NONE OF OUR PEOPLE MUST DIE BY OUR HAND.
FIRE OVER THEIR HEADS. FRIGHTEN THEM OFF
STOP! I HAVE ORDERS TO SHOOT LOOTERS.
YE DO NOT!
LET HER GO! YOU SHINNERS CAN CLEAR OFF!
PUT IT BACK OR I'LL SHOOT!

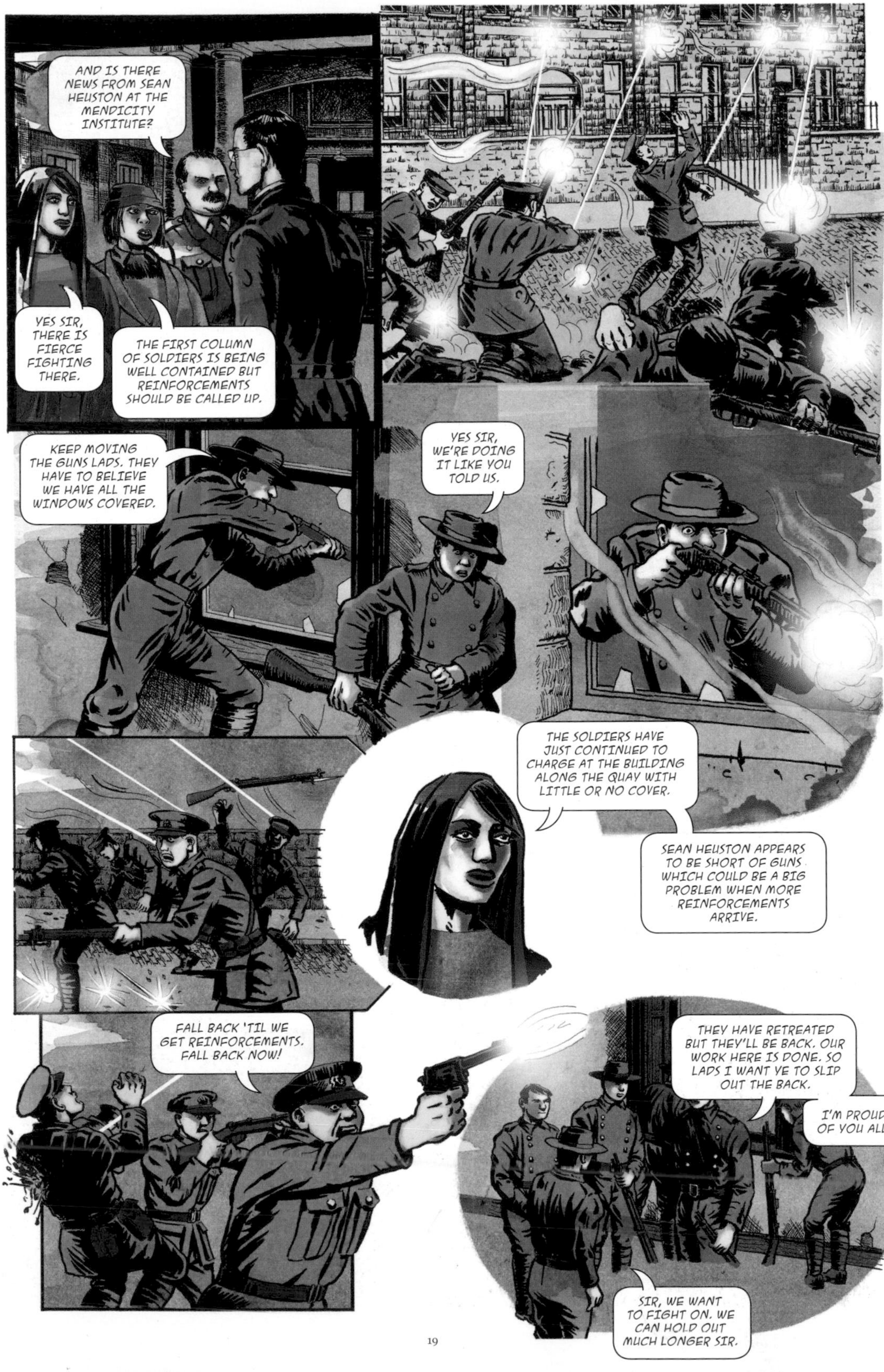
AND IS THERE NEWS FROM SEAN HEUSTON AT THE MENDICITY INSTITUTE?
YES SIR, THERE IS FIERCE FIGHTING THERE.
THE FIRST COLUMN OF SOLDIERS IS BEING WELL CONTAINED BUT REINFORCEMENTS SHOULD BE CALLED UP.
KEEP MOVING THE GUNS LADS. THEY HAVE TO BELIEVE WE HAVE ALL THE WINDOWS COVERED.
YES SIR, WE'RE DOING IT LIKE YOU TOLD US.
THE SOLDIERS HAVE JUST CONTINUED TO CHARGE AT THE BUILDING ALONG THE QUAY WITH LITTLE OR NO COVER.
SEAN HEUSTON APPEARS TO BE SHORT OF GUNS WHICH COULD BE A BIG PROBLEM WHEN MORE REINFORCEMENTS ARRIVE.
FALL BACK 'TIL WE GET REINFORCEMENTS. FALL BACK NOW!
THEY HAVE RETREATED BUT THEY'LL BE BACK. OUR WORK HERE IS DONE. SO LADS I WANT YE TO SLIP OUT THE BACK.
I'M PROUD OF YOU ALL.
SIR, WE WANT TO FIGHT ON. WE CAN HOLD OUT MUCH LONGER SIR.

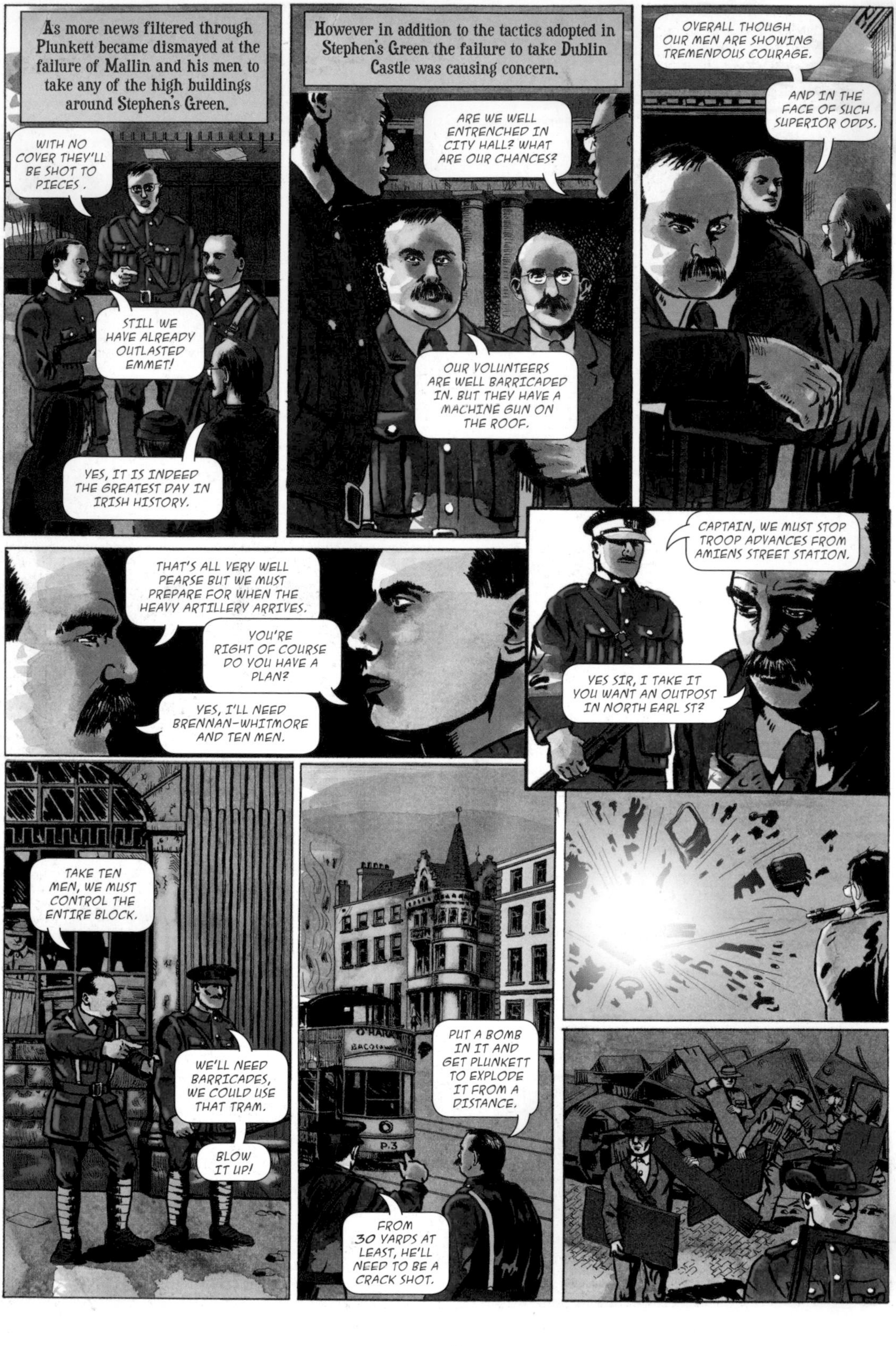
As more news filtered through Plunkett became dismayed at the failure of Mallin and his men to take any of the high buildings around Stephen's Green.
WITH NO COVER THEY'LL BE SHOT TO PIECES .
STILL WE HAVE ALREADY OUTLASTED EMMET!
YES, IT IS INDEED THE GREATEST DAY IN IRISH HISTORY.
However in addition to the tactics adopted in Stephen's Green the failure to take Dublin Castle was causing concern.
ARE WE WELL ENTRENCHED IN CITY HALL? WHAT ARE OUR CHANCES?
OUR VOLUNTEERS ARE WELL BARRICADED IN. BUT THEY HAVE A MACHINE GUN ON THE ROOF.
OVERALL THOUGH OUR MEN ARE SHOWING TREMENDOUS COURAGE.
AND IN THE FACE OF SUCH SUPERIOR ODDS.
THAT'S ALL VERY WELL PEARSE BUT WE MUST PREPARE FOR WHEN THE HEAVY ARTILLERY ARRIVES.
YOU'RE RIGHT OF COURSE DO YOU HAVE A PLAN?
YES, I'LL NEED BRENNAN-WHITMORE AND TEN MEN.
CAPTAIN, WE MUST STOP TROOP ADVANCES FROM AMIENS STREET STATION.
YES SIR, I TAKE IT YOU WANT AN OUTPOST IN NORTH EARL ST?
TAKE TEN MEN, WE MUST CONTROL THE ENTIRE BLOCK.
WE'LL NEED BARRICADES, WE COULD USE THAT TRAM.
BLOW IT UP!
PUT A BOMB IN IT AND GET PLUNKETT TO EXPLODE IT FROM A DISTANCE.
FROM 30 YARDS AT LEAST, HE'LL NEED TO BE A CRACK SHOT.

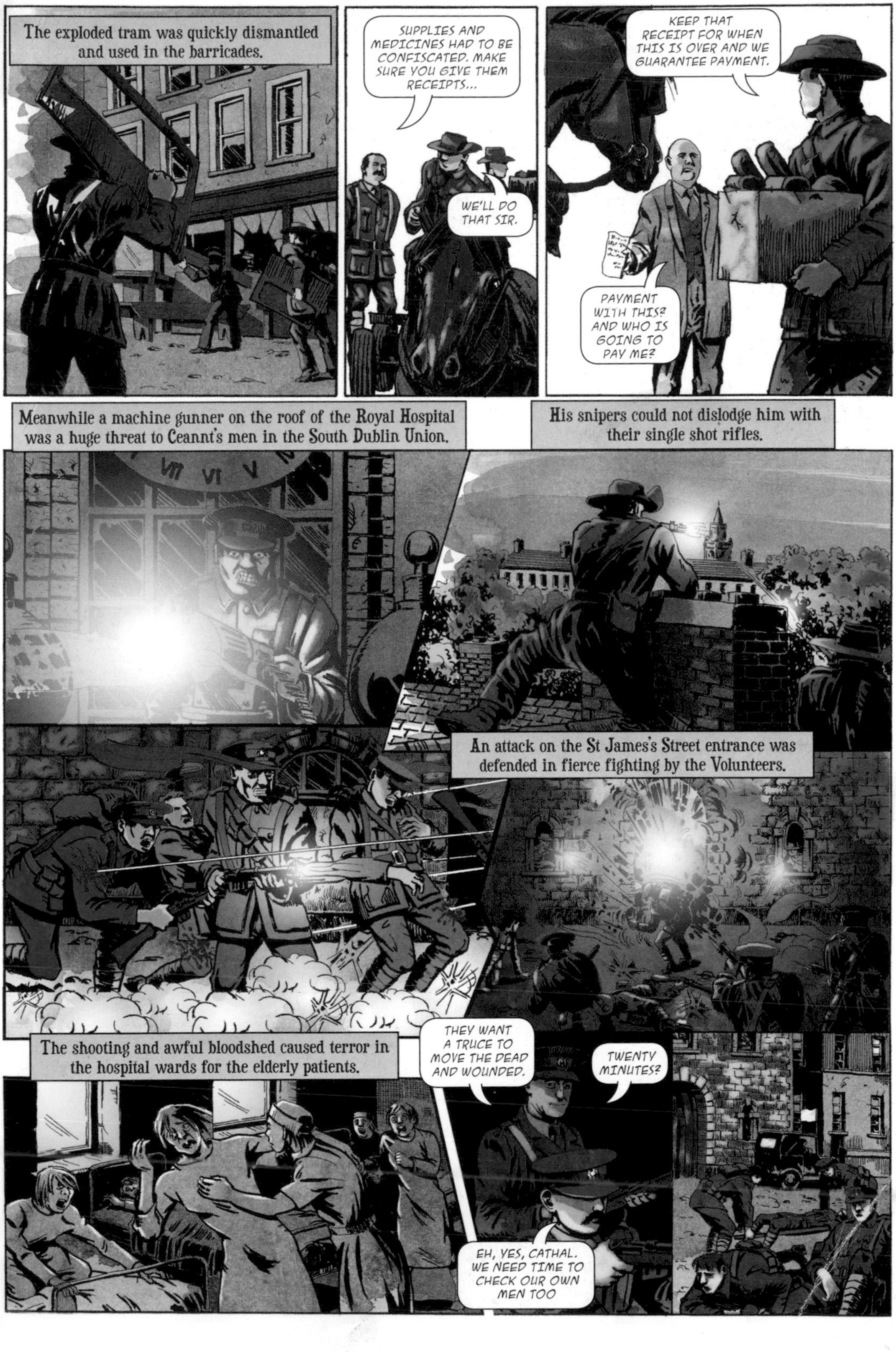
The exploded tram was quickly dismantled and used in the barricades.
SUPPLIES AND MEDICINES HAD TO BE CONFISCATED. MAKE SURE YOU GIVE THEM RECEIPTS...
WE'LL DO THAT SIR.
KEEP THAT RECEIPT FOR WHEN THIS IS OVER AND WE GUARANTEE PAYMENT.
PAYMENT WITH THIS? AND WHO IS GOING TO PAY ME?
Meanwhile a machine gunner on the roof of the Royal Hospital was a huge threat to Ceannt's men in the South Dublin Union.
His snipers could not dislodge him with their single shot rifles.
An attack on the St James's Street entrance was defended in fierce fighting by the Volunteers.
The shooting and awful bloodshed caused terror in the hospital wards for the elderly patients.
THEY WANT A TRUCE TO MOVE THE DEAD AND WOUNDED.
TWENTY MINUTES?
EH, YES, CATHAL. WE NEED TIME TO CHECK OUR OWN MEN TOO

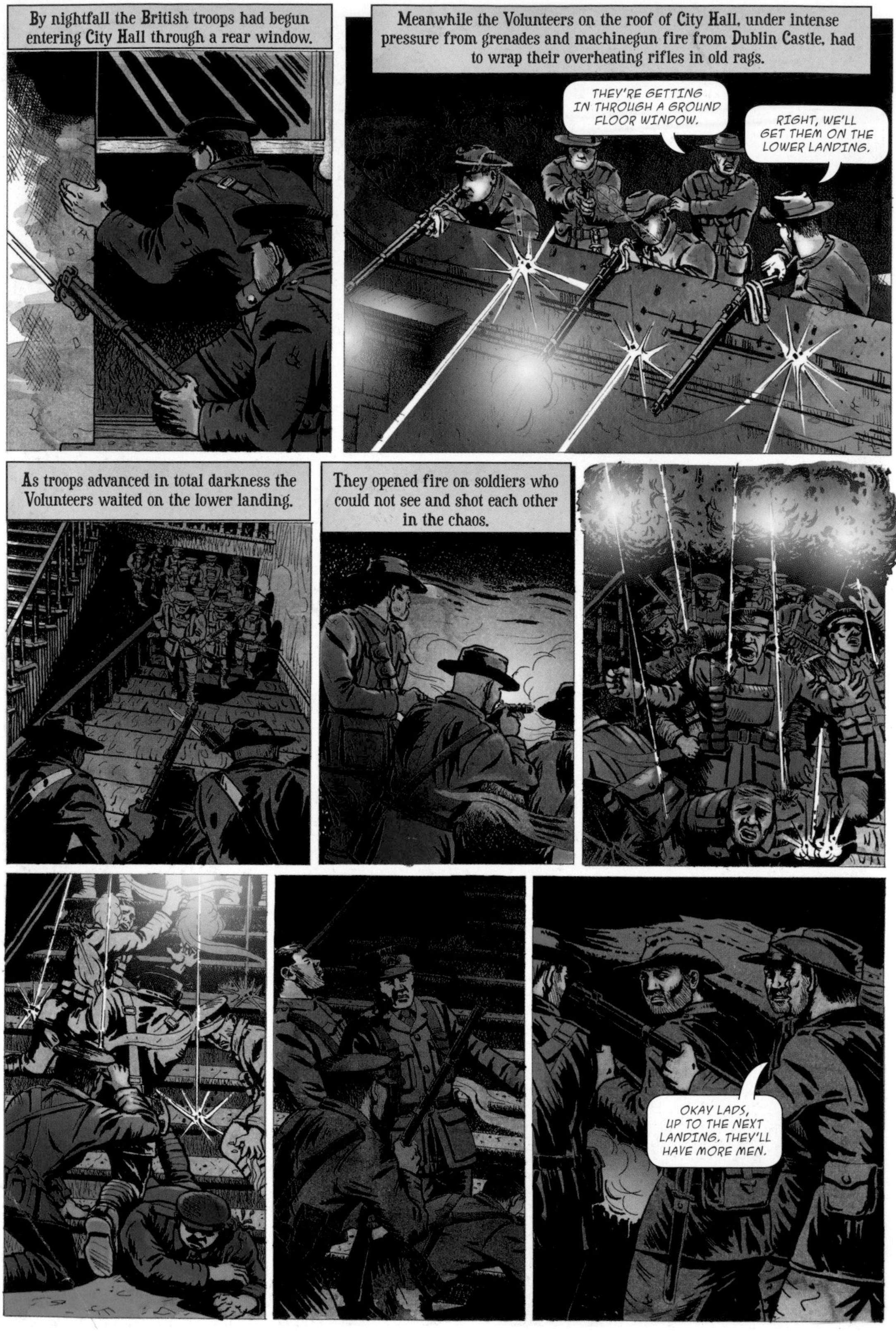
By nightfall the British troops had begun entering City Hall through a rear window.
Meanwhile the Volunteers on the roof of City Hall, under intense pressure from grenades and machinegun fire from Dublin Castle, had to wrap their overheating rifles in old rags.
THEY'RE GETTING IN THROUGH A GROUND FLOOR WINDOW.
RIGHT, WE'LL GET THEM ON THE LOWER LANDING.
As troops advanced in total darkness the Volunteers waited on the lower landing.
They opened fire on soldiers who could not see and shot each other in the chaos.
OKAY LADS, UP TO THE NEXT LANDING. THEY'LL HAVE MORE MEN.

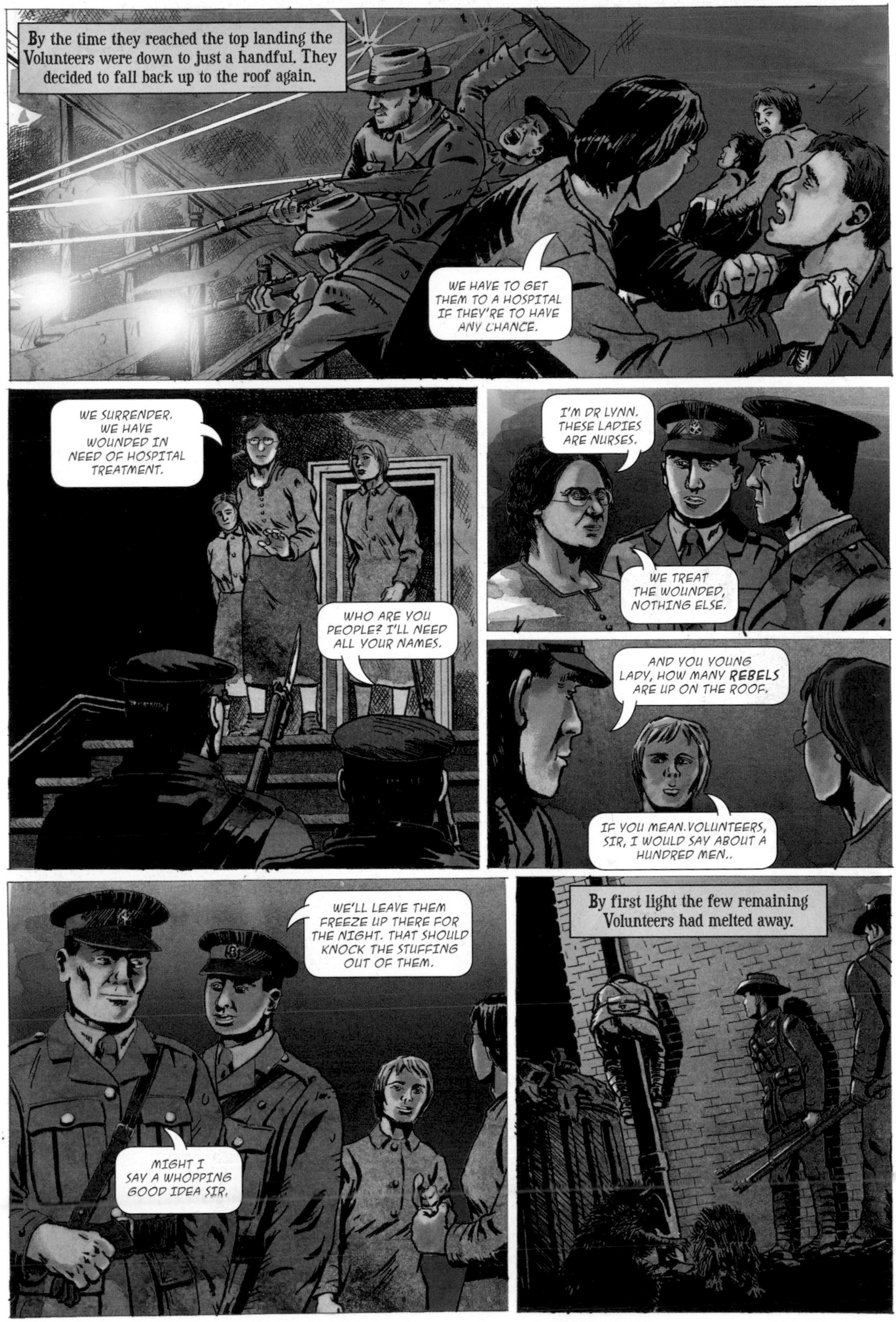
By the time they reached the top landing the Volunteers were down to just a handful. They decided to fall back up to the roof again.
WE HAVE TO GET THEM TO A HOSPITAL IF THEY'RE TO HAVE ANY CHANCE.
WE SURRENDER. WE HAVE WOUNDED IN NEED OF HOSPITAL TREATMENT.
WHO ARE YOU PEOPLE? I'LL NEED ALL YOUR NAMES.
I'M DR LYNN. THESE LADIES ARE NURSES.
WE TREAT THE WOUNDED, NOTHING ELSE.
AND YOU YOUNG LADY, HOW MANY REBELS ARE UP ON THE ROOF.
IF YOU MEAN.VOLUNTEERS, SIR, I WOULD SAY ABOUT A HUNDRED MEN..
WE'LL LEAVE THEM FREEZE UP THERE FOR THE NIGHT. THAT SHOULD KNOCK THE STUFFING OUT OF THEM.
MIGHT I SAY A WHOPPING GOOD IDEA SIR.
By first light the few remaining Volunteers had melted away.

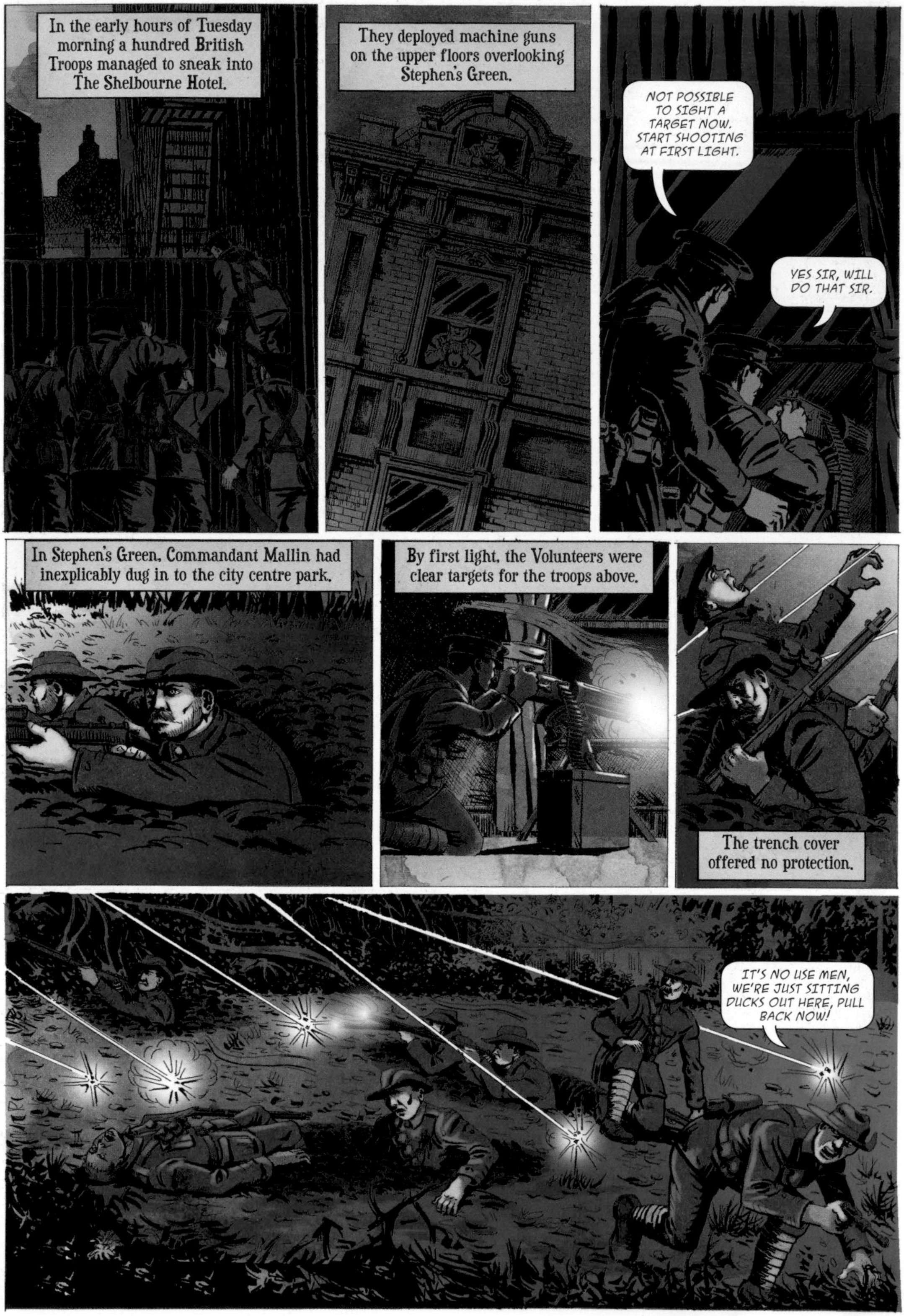
In the early hours of Tuesday morning a hundred British Troops managed to sneak into The Shelbourne Hotel.
They deployed machine guns on the upper floors overlooking Stephen's Green.
NOT POSSIBLE TO SIGHT A TARGET NOW. START SHOOTING AT FIRST LIGHT.
YES SIR, WILL DO THAT SIR.
In Stephen's Green, Commandant Mallin had inexplicably dug in to the city centre park.
By first light, the Volunteers were clear targets for the troops above.
The trench cover offered no protection.
IT'S NO USE MEN, WE'RE JUST SITTING DUCKS OUT HERE, PULL BACK NOW!

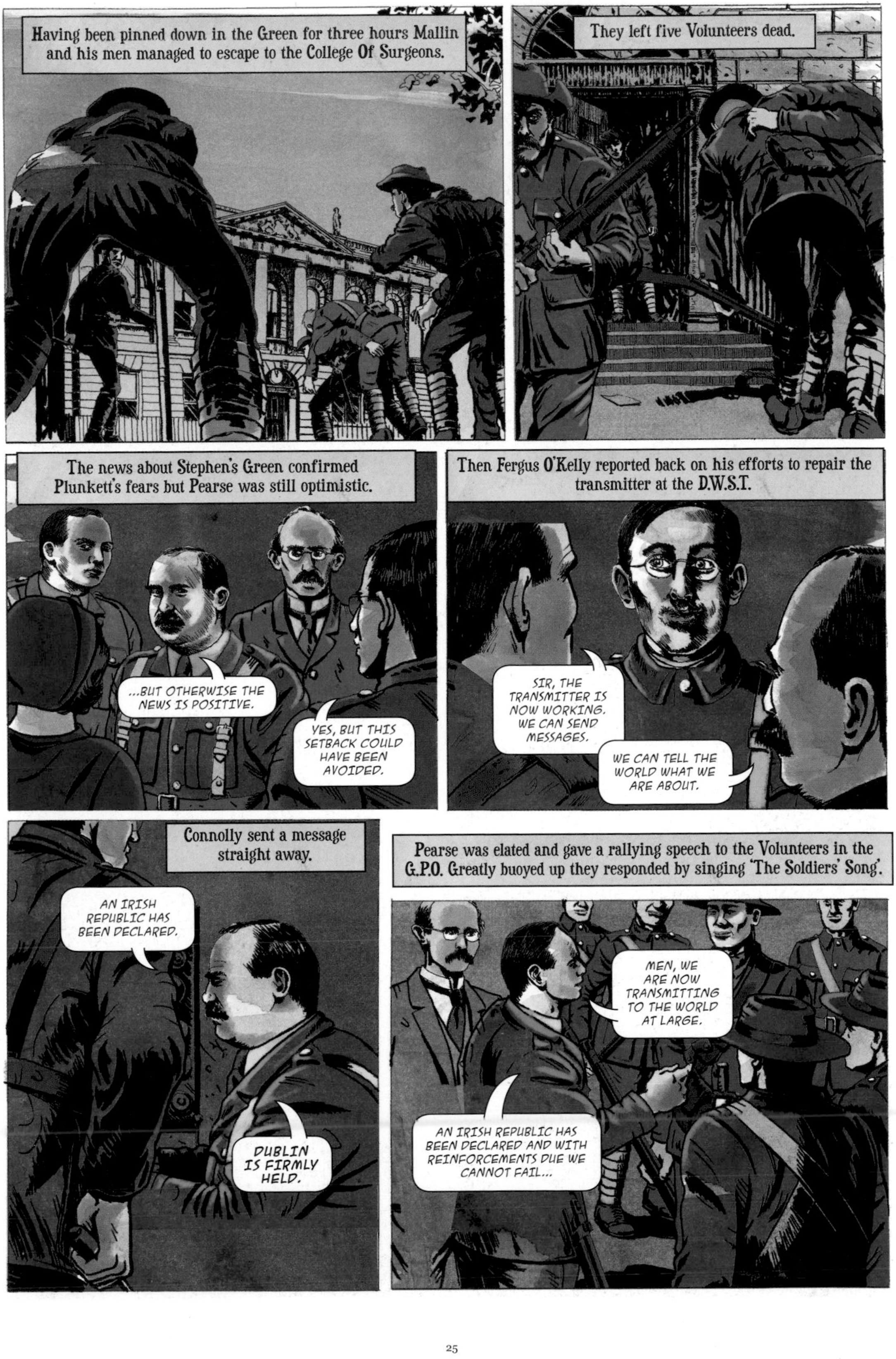
Having been pinned down in the Green for three hours Mallin and his men managed to escape to the College Of Surgeons.
They left five Volunteers dead.
The news about Stephen's Green confirmed Plunkett's fears but Pearse was still optimistic.
...BUT OTHERWISE THE NEWS IS POSITIVE.
YES, BUT THIS SETBACK COULD HAVE BEEN AVOIDED.
Then Fergus O'Kelly reported back on his efforts to repair the transmitter at the D.W.S.T.
SIR, THE TRANSMITTER IS NOW WORKING. WE CAN SEND MESSAGES.
WE CAN TELL THE WORLD WHAT WE ARE ABOUT.
Connolly sent a message straight away.
AN IRISH REPUBLIC HAS BEEN DECLARED.
DUBLIN IS FIRMLY HELD.
Pearse was elated and gave a rallying speech to the Volunteers in the G.P.O. Greatly buoyed up they responded by singing 'The Soldiers' Song'.
MEN, WE ARE NOW TRANSMITTING TO THE WORLD AT LARGE.
AN IRISH REPUBLIC HAS BEEN DECLARED AND WITH REINFORCEMENTS DUE WE CANNOT FAIL...

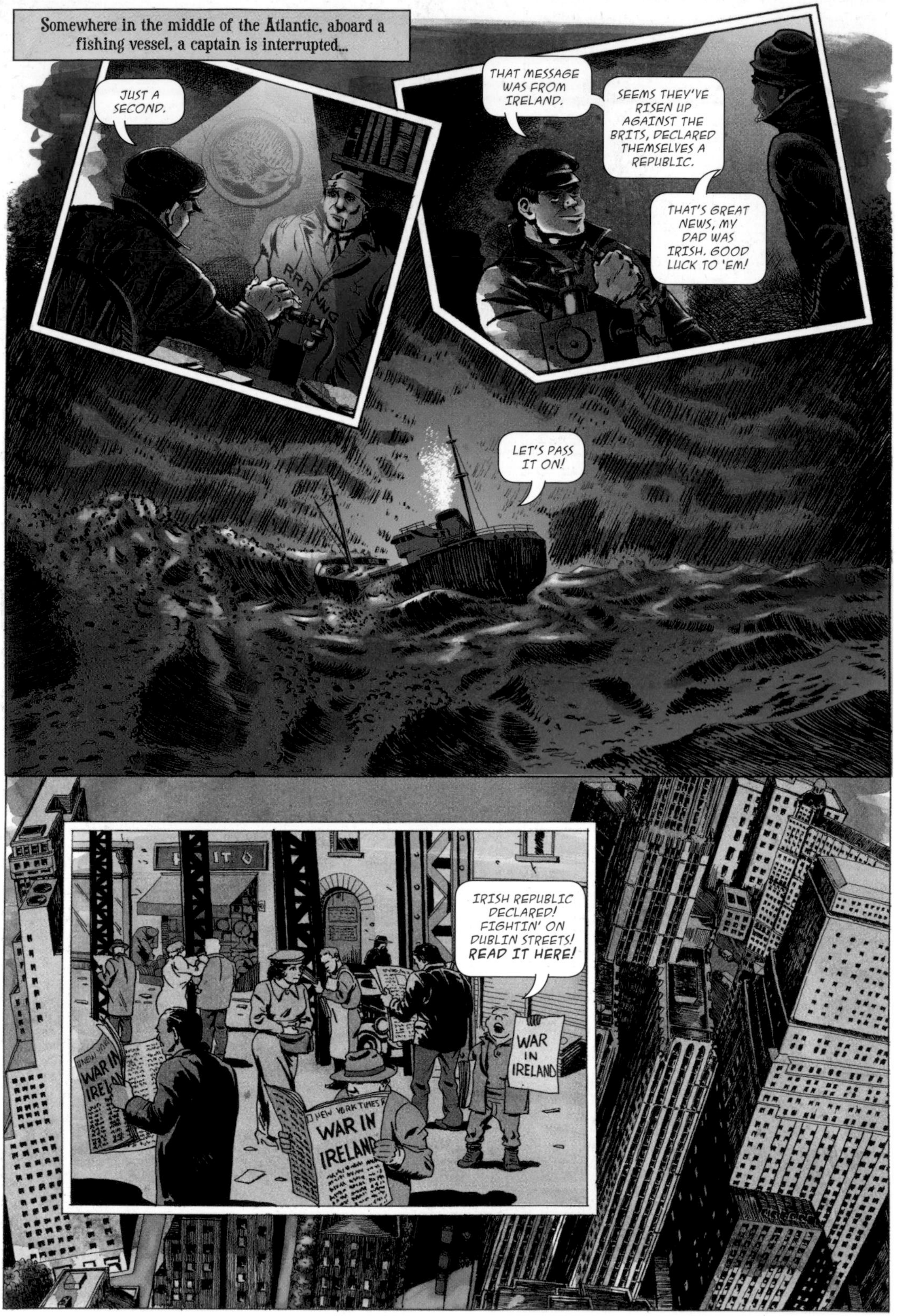
Somewhere in the middle of the Atlantic, aboard a fishing vessel, a captain is interrupted...
JUST A SECOND.
RRRING
THAT MESSAGE WAS FROM IRELAND.
SEEMS THEY'VE RISEN UP AGAINST THE BRITS, DECLARED THEMSELVES A REPUBLIC.
THAT'S GREAT NEWS, MY DAD WAS IRISH. GOOD LUCK TO 'EM!
LET'S PASS IT ON!
IRISH REPUBLIC DECLARED! FIGHTIN' ON DUBLIN STREETS! READ IT HERE!
WAR IN IRELAND
WAR IN IRELAND
NEW YORK TIMES
WAR IN IRELAND

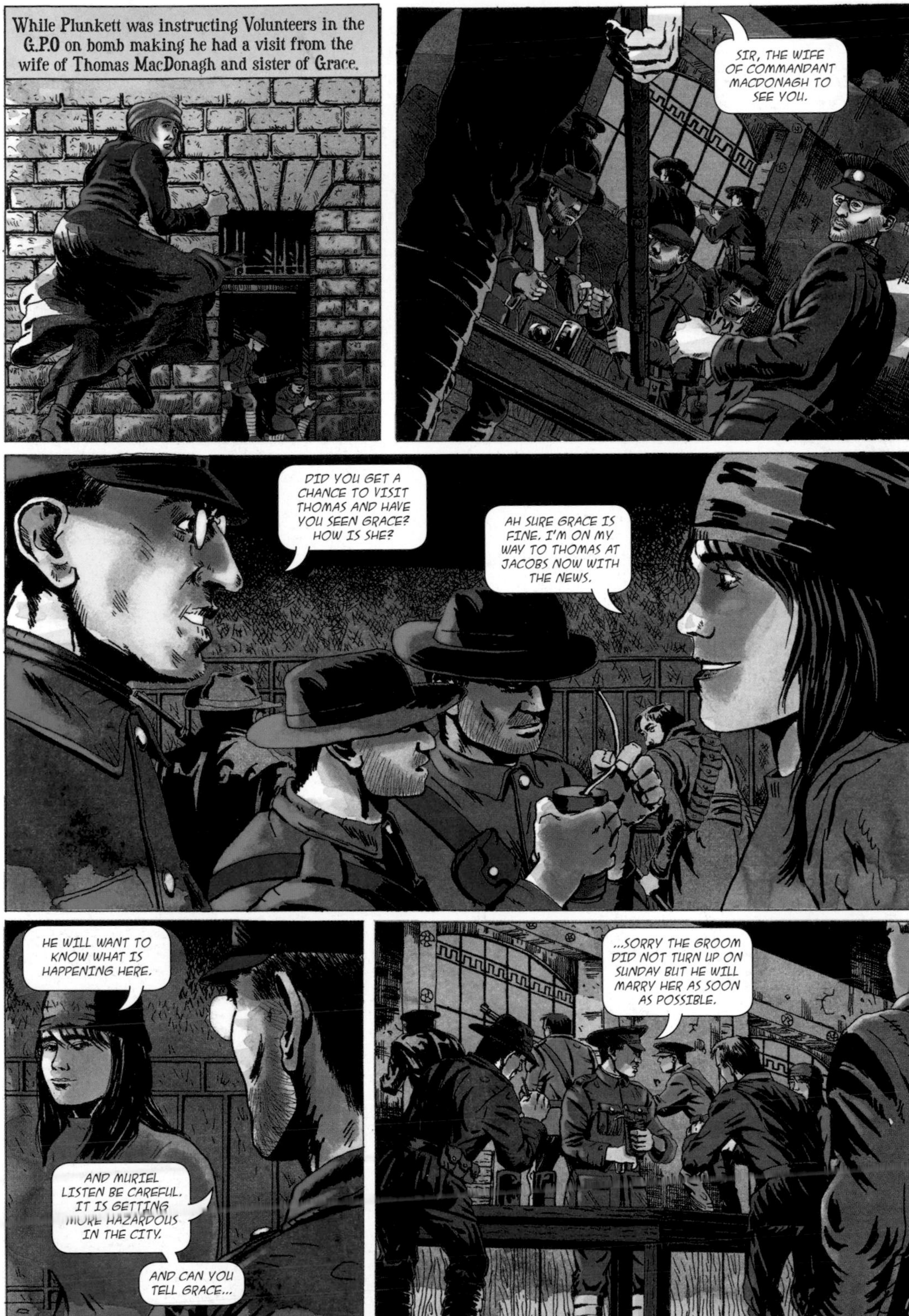

While Plunkett was instructing Volunteers in the G.P.O on bomb making he had a visit from the wife of Thomas MacDonagh and sister of Grace.
SIR, THE WIFE OF COMMANDANT MACDONAGH TO SEE YOU.
DID YOU GET A CHANCE TO VISIT THOMAS AND HAVE YOU SEEN GRACE? HOW IS SHE?
AH SURE GRACE IS FINE. I'M ON MY WAY TO THOMAS AT JACOBS NOW WITH THE NEWS.
HE WILL WANT TO KNOW WHAT IS HAPPENING HERE.
AND MURIEL LISTEN BE CAREFUL. IT IS GETTING MORE HAZARDOUS IN THE CITY.
AND CAN YOU TELL GRACE...
...SORRY THE GROOM DID NOT TURN UP ON SUNDAY BUT HE WILL MARRY HER AS SOON AS POSSIBLE.

Wednesday 26th April, 8AM

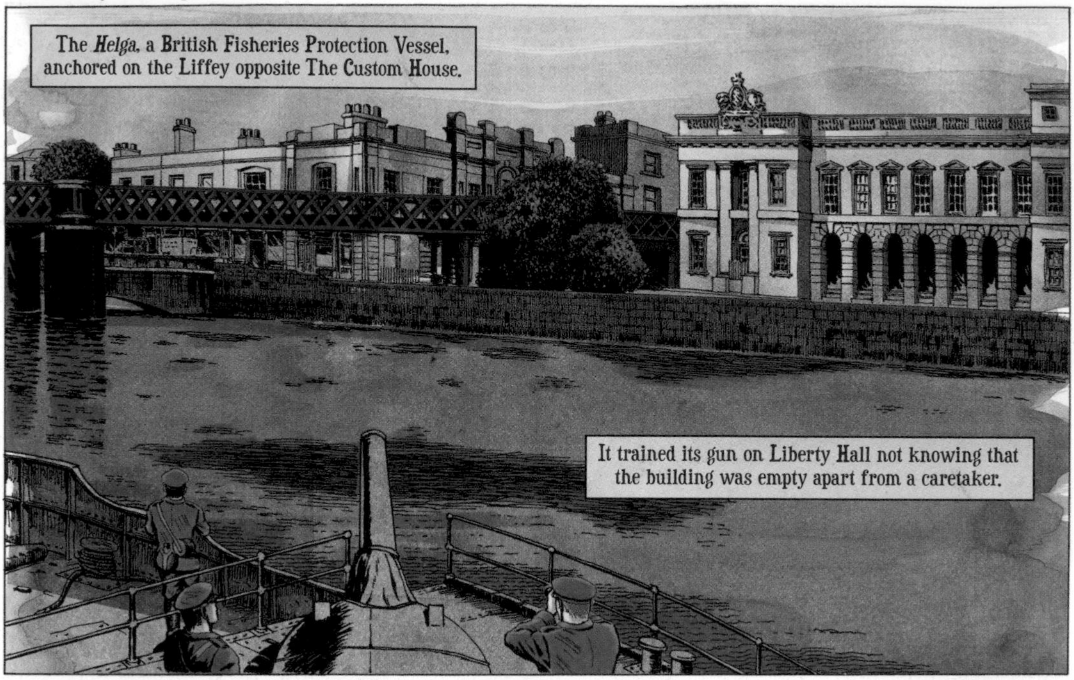
The *Helga*, a British Fisheries Protection Vessel, anchored on the Liffey opposite The Custom House.
It trained its gun on Liberty Hall not knowing that the building was empty apart from a caretaker.

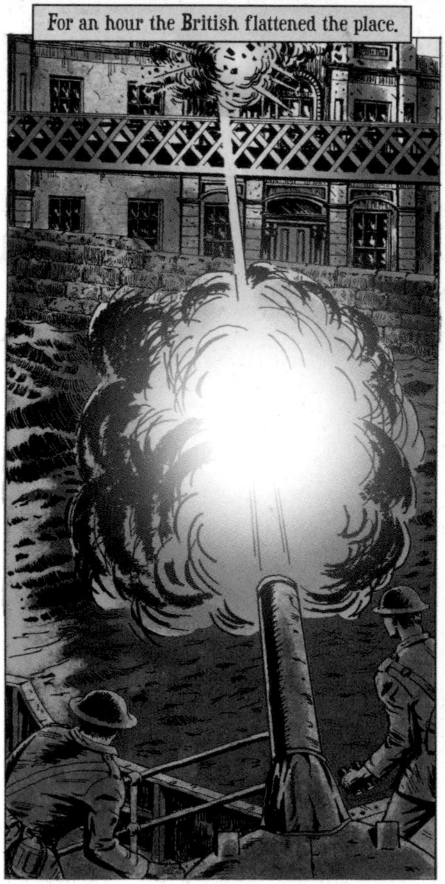
For an hour the British flattened the place.

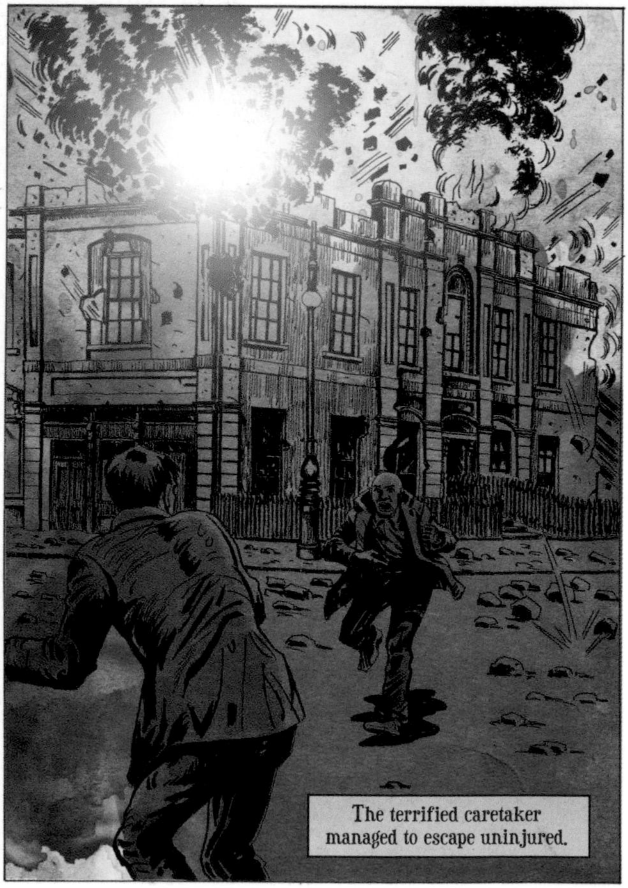
The terrified caretaker managed to escape uninjured.

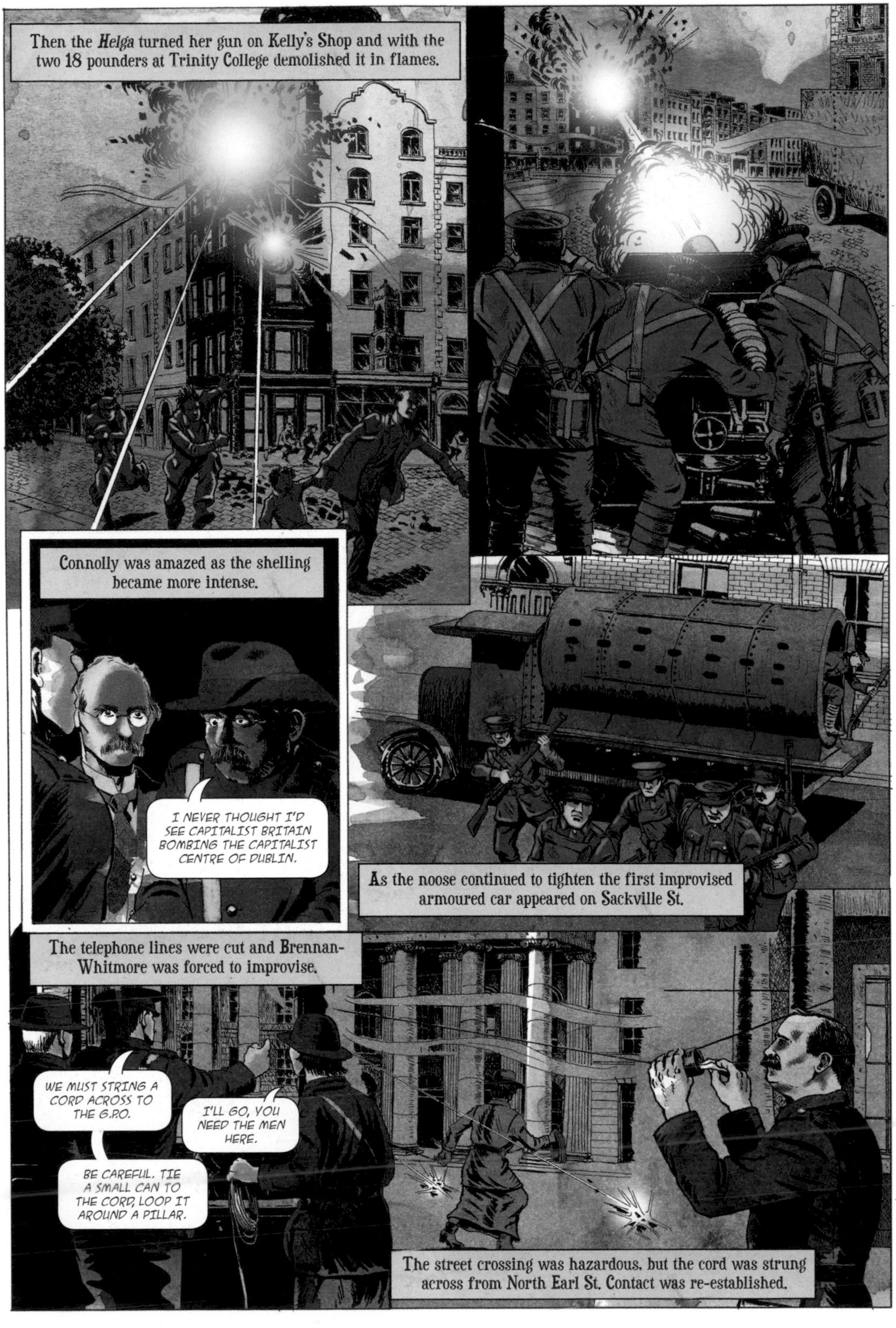

Then the *Helga* turned her gun on Kelly's Shop and with the two 18 pounders at Trinity College demolished it in flames.
Connolly was amazed as the shelling became more intense.
I NEVER THOUGHT I'D SEE CAPITALIST BRITAIN BOMBING THE CAPITALIST CENTRE OF DUBLIN.
As the noose continued to tighten the first improvised armoured car appeared on Sackville St.
The telephone lines were cut and Brennan-Whitmore was forced to improvise.
WE MUST STRING A CORD ACROSS TO THE G.P.O.
I'LL GO, YOU NEED THE MEN HERE.
BE CAREFUL. TIE A SMALL CAN TO THE CORD, LOOP IT AROUND A PILLAR.
The street crossing was hazardous, but the cord was strung across from North Earl St. Contact was re-established.

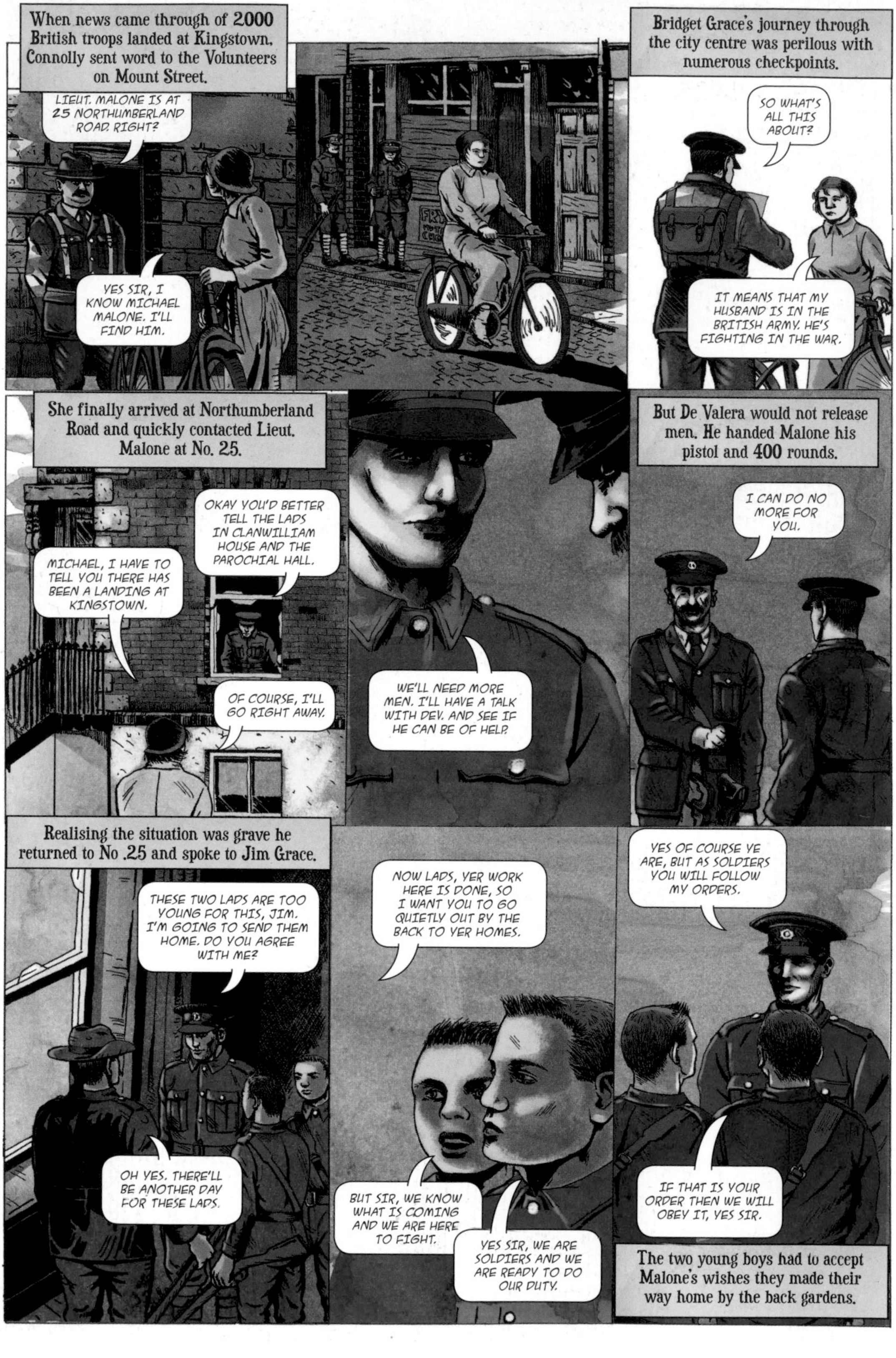
When news came through of 2000 British troops landed at Kingstown, Connolly sent word to the Volunteers on Mount Street.
LIEUT. MALONE IS AT 25 NORTHUMBERLAND ROAD. RIGHT?
YES SIR, I KNOW MICHAEL MALONE. I'LL FIND HIM.
Bridget Grace's journey through the city centre was perilous with numerous checkpoints.
SO WHAT'S ALL THIS ABOUT?
IT MEANS THAT MY HUSBAND IS IN THE BRITISH ARMY. HE'S FIGHTING IN THE WAR.
She finally arrived at Northumberland Road and quickly contacted Lieut. Malone at No. 25.
MICHAEL, I HAVE TO TELL YOU THERE HAS BEEN A LANDING AT KINGSTOWN.
OKAY YOU'D BETTER TELL THE LADS IN CLANWILLIAM HOUSE AND THE PAROCHIAL HALL.
OF COURSE, I'LL GO RIGHT AWAY.
WE'LL NEED MORE MEN. I'LL HAVE A TALK WITH DEV. AND SEE IF HE CAN BE OF HELP.
But De Valera would not release men. He handed Malone his pistol and 400 rounds.
I CAN DO NO MORE FOR YOU.
Realising the situation was grave he returned to No .25 and spoke to Jim Grace.
THESE TWO LADS ARE TOO YOUNG FOR THIS, JIM. I'M GOING TO SEND THEM HOME. DO YOU AGREE WITH ME?
OH YES. THERE'LL BE ANOTHER DAY FOR THESE LADS.
NOW LADS, YER WORK HERE IS DONE, SO I WANT YOU TO GO QUIETLY OUT BY THE BACK TO YER HOMES.
BUT SIR, WE KNOW WHAT IS COMING AND WE ARE HERE TO FIGHT.
YES SIR, WE ARE SOLDIERS AND WE ARE READY TO DO OUR DUTY.
YES OF COURSE YE ARE, BUT AS SOLDIERS YOU WILL FOLLOW MY ORDERS.
IF THAT IS YOUR ORDER THEN WE WILL OBEY IT, YES SIR.
The two young boys had to accept Malone's wishes they made their way home by the back gardens.

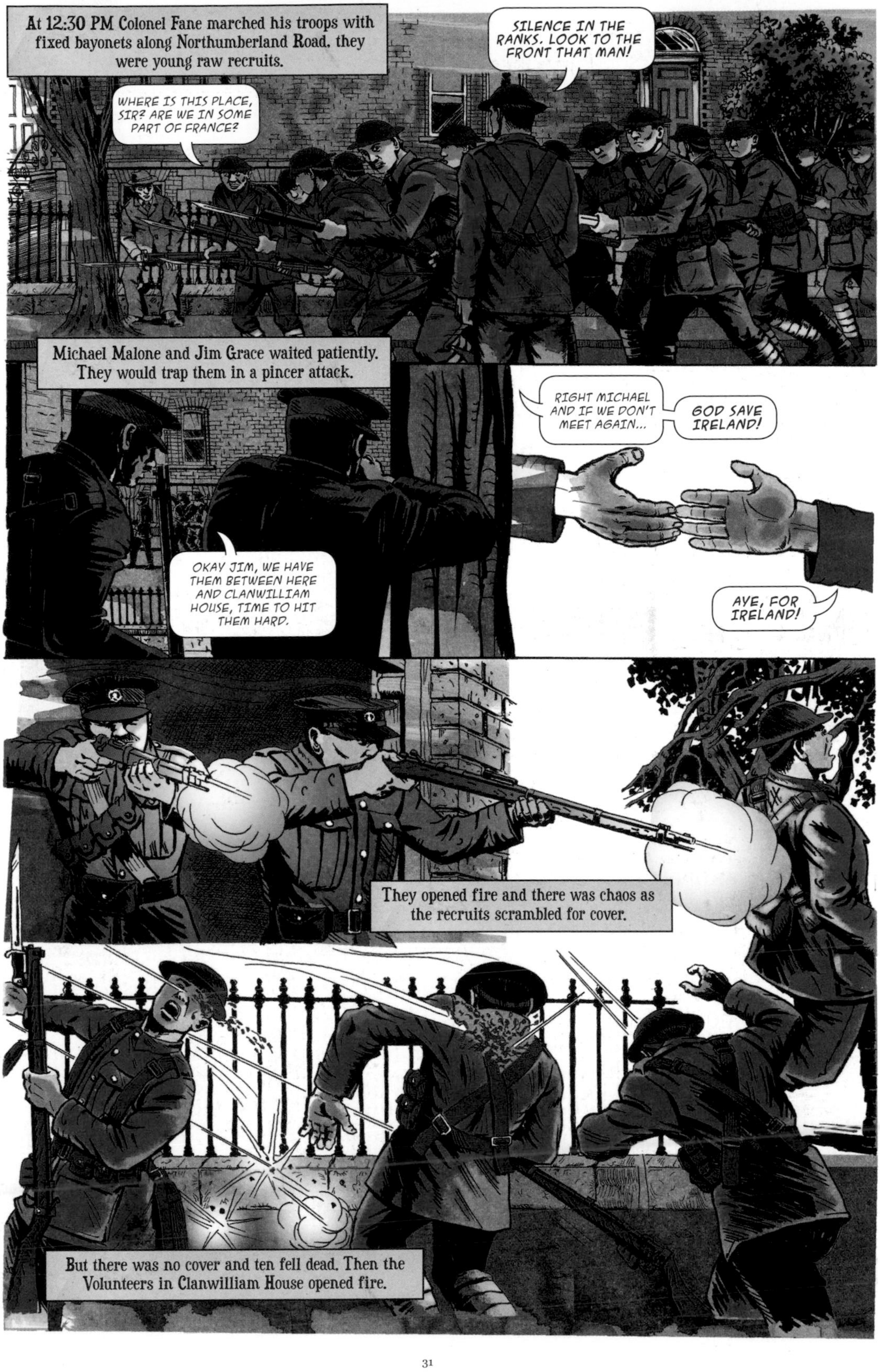
At 12:30 PM Colonel Fane marched his troops with fixed bayonets along Northumberland Road, they were young raw recruits.
SILENCE IN THE RANKS. LOOK TO THE FRONT THAT MAN!
WHERE IS THIS PLACE, SIR? ARE WE IN SOME PART OF FRANCE?
Michael Malone and Jim Grace waited patiently. They would trap them in a pincer attack.
OKAY JIM, WE HAVE THEM BETWEEN HERE AND CLANWILLIAM HOUSE, TIME TO HIT THEM HARD.
RIGHT MICHAEL AND IF WE DON'T MEET AGAIN...
GOD SAVE IRELAND!
AYE, FOR IRELAND!
They opened fire and there was chaos as the recruits scrambled for cover.
But there was no cover and ten fell dead. Then the Volunteers in Clanwilliam House opened fire.

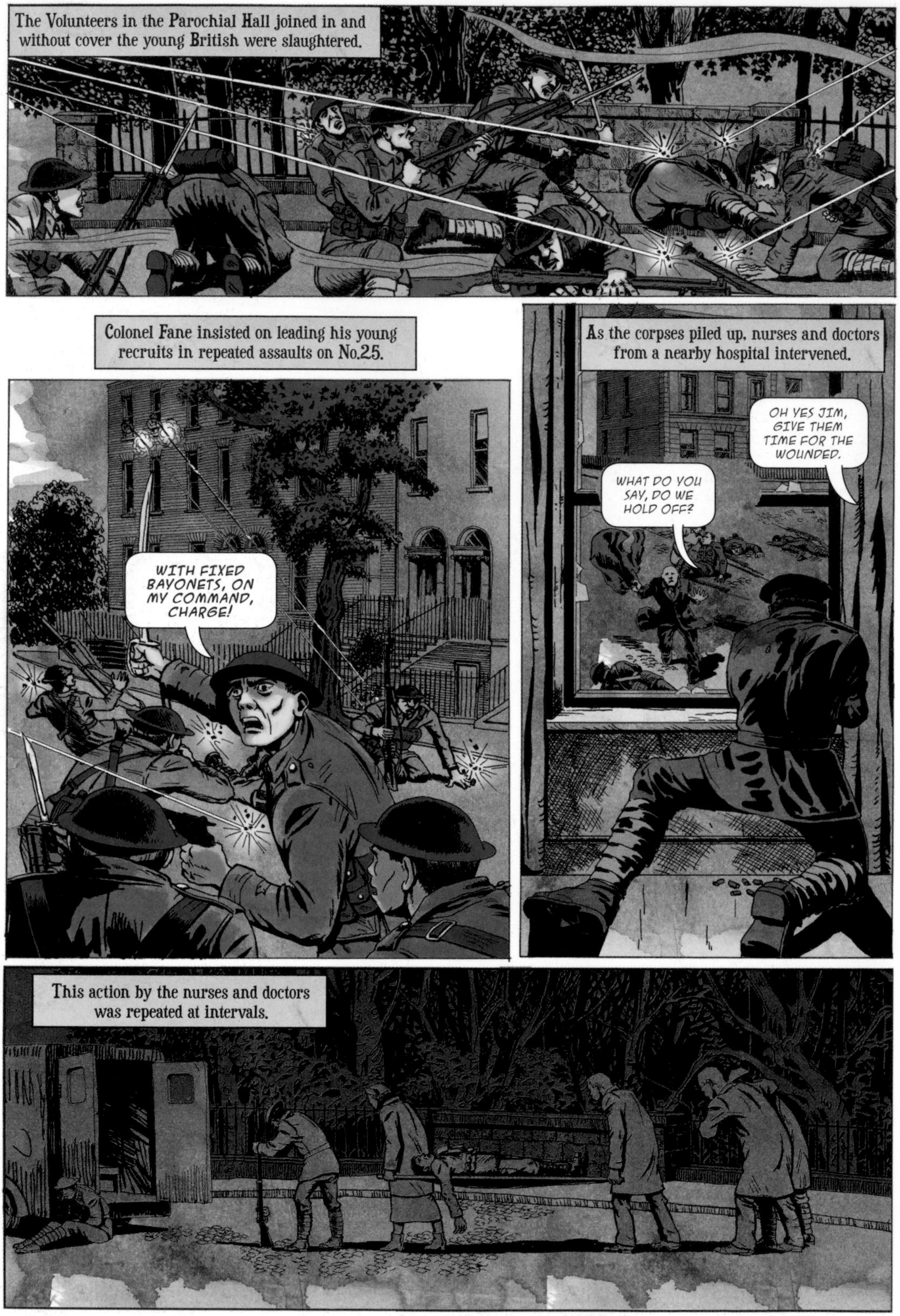
The Volunteers in the Parochial Hall joined in and without cover the young British were slaughtered.
Colonel Fane insisted on leading his young recruits in repeated assaults on No.25.
WITH FIXED BAYONETS, ON MY COMMAND, CHARGE!
As the corpses piled up, nurses and doctors from a nearby hospital intervened.
WHAT DO YOU SAY, DO WE HOLD OFF?
OH YES JIM, GIVE THEM TIME FOR THE WOUNDED.
This action by the nurses and doctors was repeated at intervals.

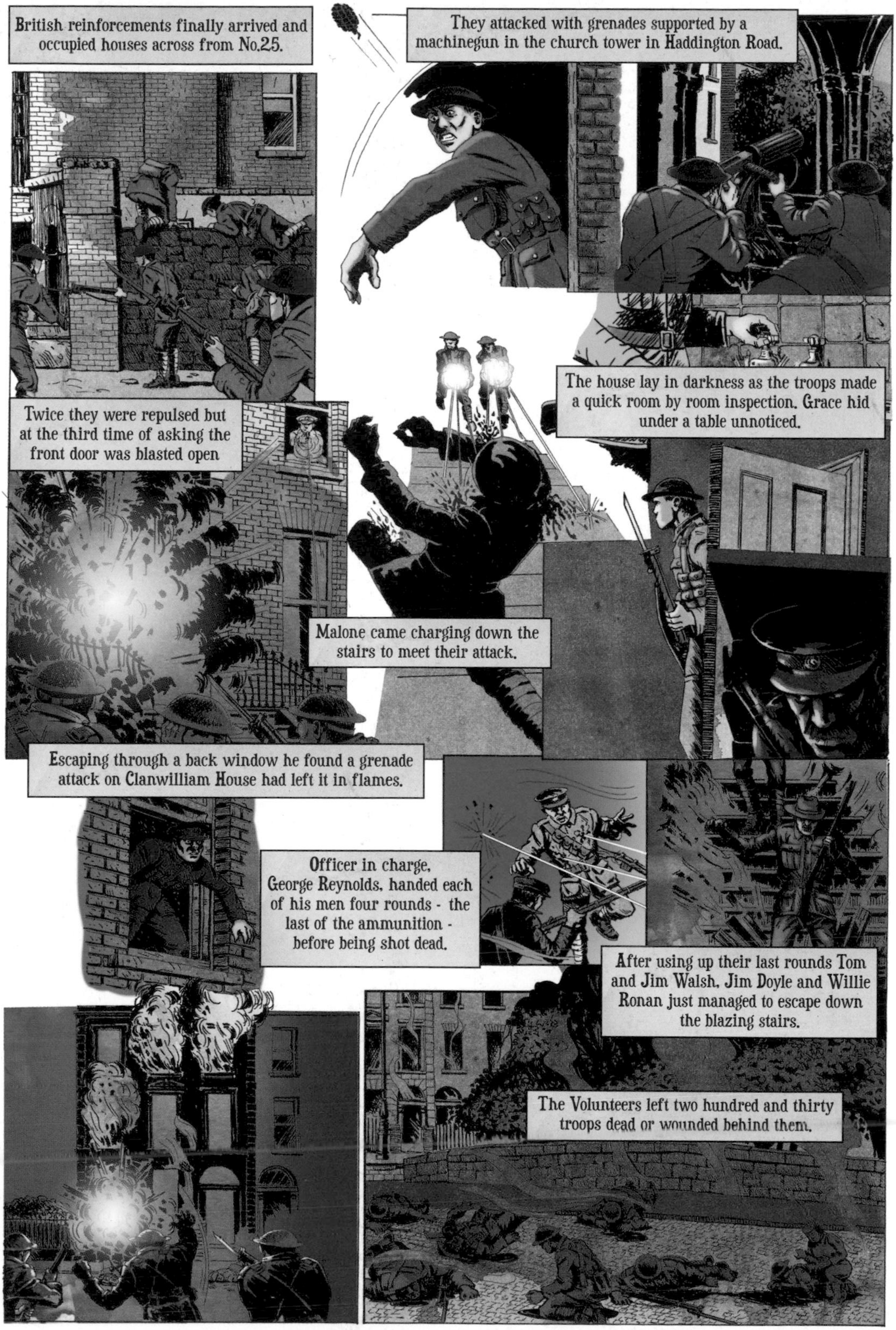
British reinforcements finally arrived and occupied houses across from No.25.
They attacked with grenades supported by a machinegun in the church tower in Haddington Road.
The house lay in darkness as the troops made a quick room by room inspection. Grace hid under a table unnoticed.
Twice they were repulsed but at the third time of asking the front door was blasted open
Malone came charging down the stairs to meet their attack.
Escaping through a back window he found a grenade attack on Clanwilliam House had left it in flames.
Officer in charge, George Reynolds, handed each of his men four rounds - the last of the ammunition - before being shot dead.
After using up their last rounds Tom and Jim Walsh, Jim Doyle and Willie Ronan just managed to escape down the blazing stairs.
The Volunteers left two hundred and thirty troops dead or wounded behind them.

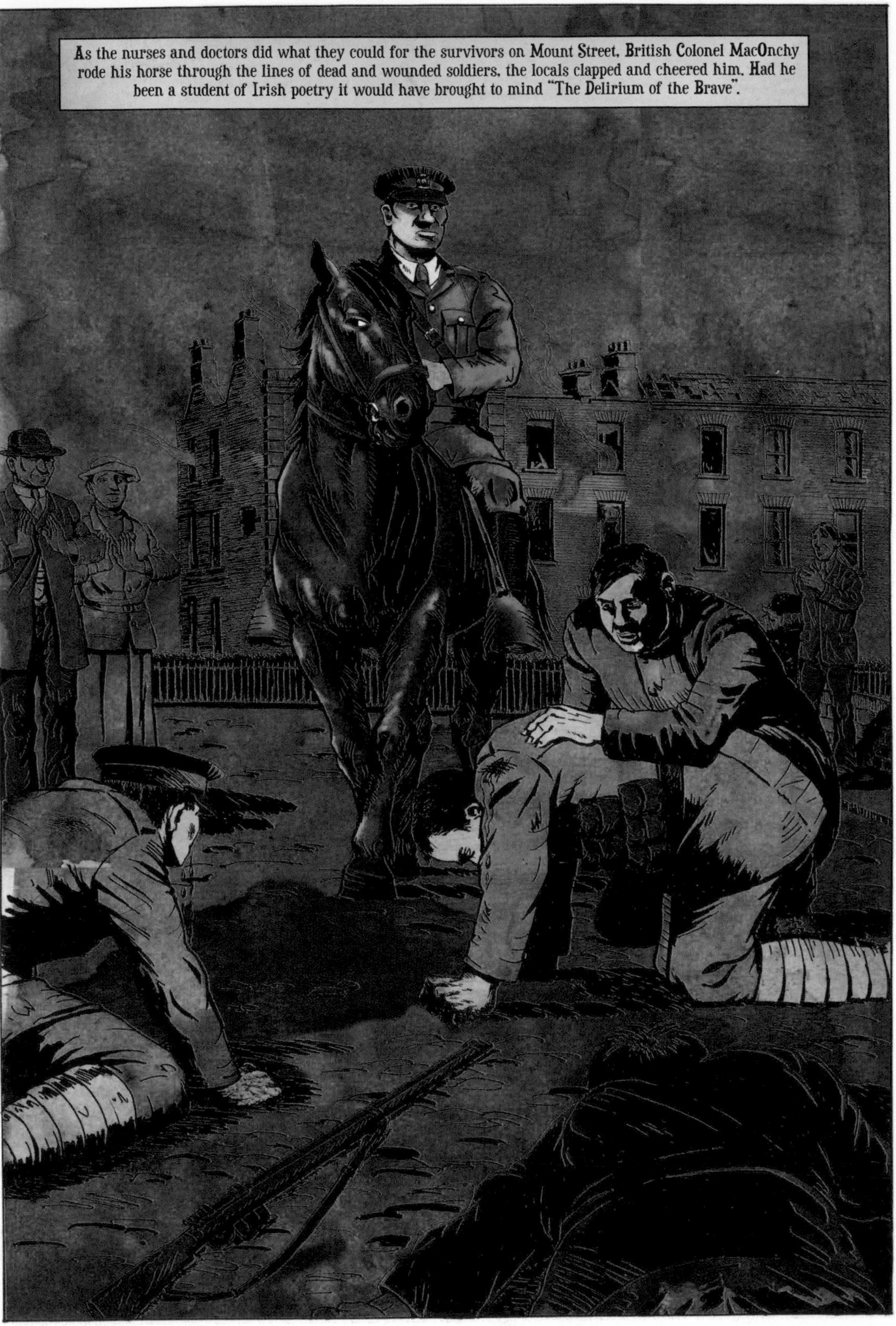
As the nurses and doctors did what they could for the survivors on Mount Street, British Colonel MacOnchy rode his horse through the lines of dead and wounded soldiers, the locals clapped and cheered him. Had he been a student of Irish poetry it would have brought to mind "The Delirium of the Brave".

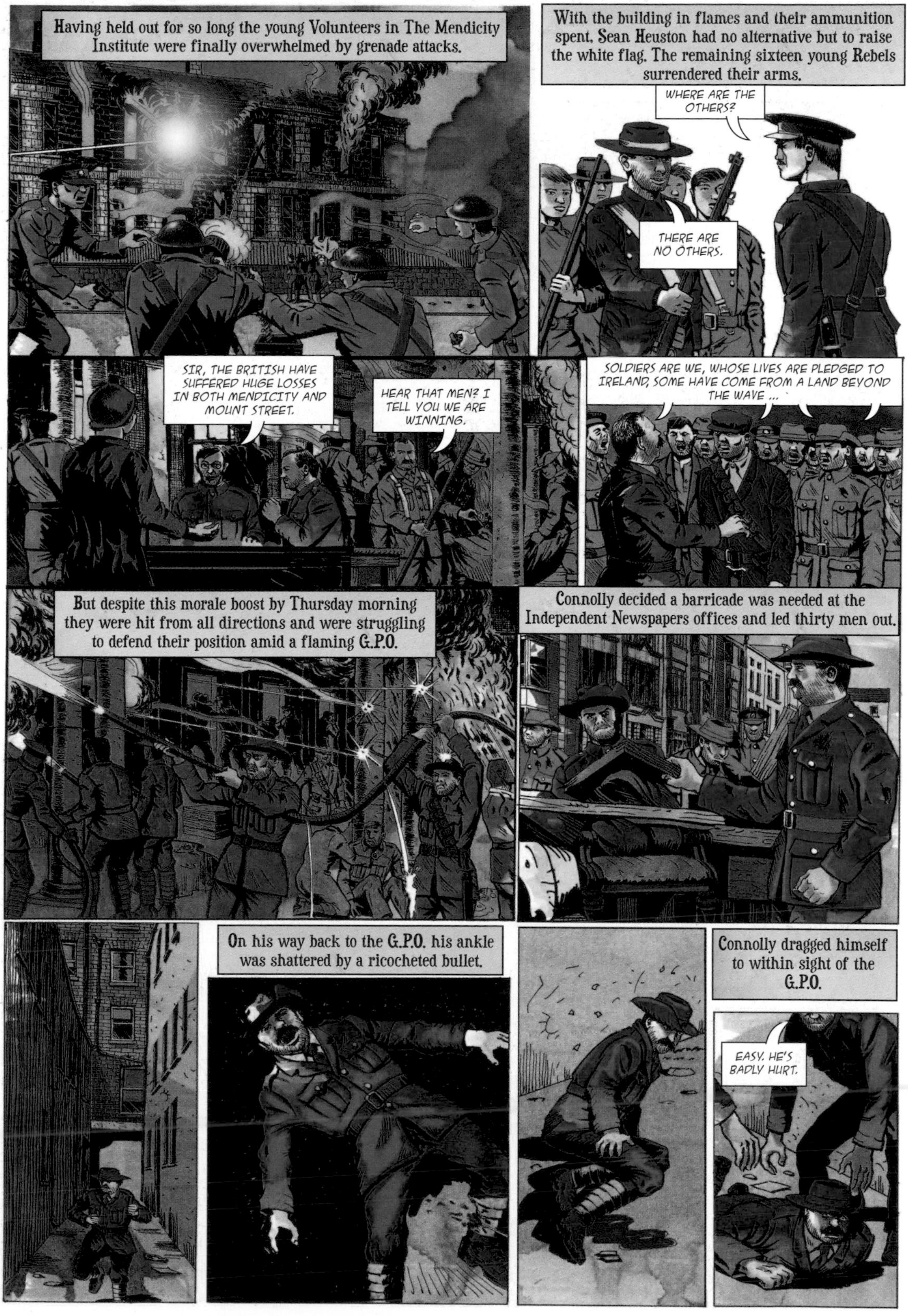
Having held out for so long the young Volunteers in The Mendicity Institute were finally overwhelmed by grenade attacks.
With the building in flames and their ammunition spent, Sean Heuston had no alternative but to raise the white flag. The remaining sixteen young Rebels surrendered their arms.
WHERE ARE THE OTHERS?
THERE ARE NO OTHERS.
SIR, THE BRITISH HAVE SUFFERED HUGE LOSSES IN BOTH MENDICITY AND MOUNT STREET.
HEAR THAT MEN? I TELL YOU WE ARE WINNING.
SOLDIERS ARE WE, WHOSE LIVES ARE PLEDGED TO IRELAND, SOME HAVE COME FROM A LAND BEYOND THE WAVE ...
But despite this morale boost by Thursday morning they were hit from all directions and were struggling to defend their position amid a flaming G.P.O.
Connolly decided a barricade was needed at the Independent Newspapers offices and led thirty men out.
On his way back to the G.P.O. his ankle was shattered by a ricocheted bullet.
Connolly dragged himself to within sight of the G.P.O.
EASY. HE'S BADLY HURT.

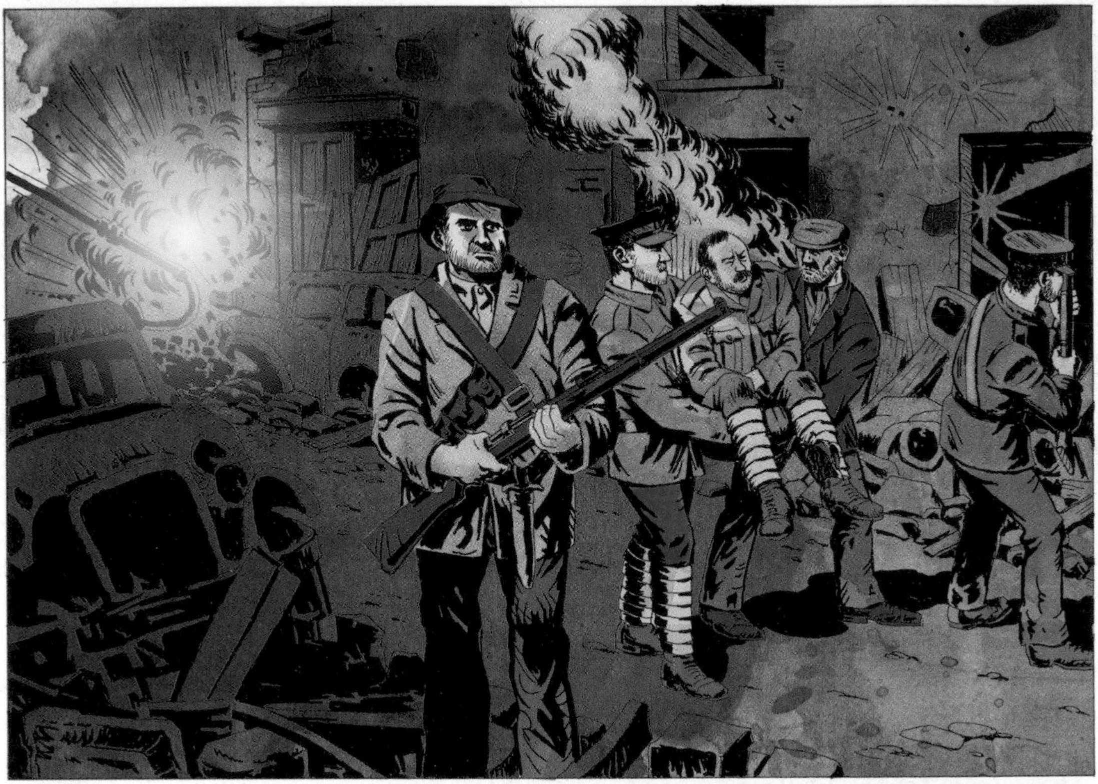

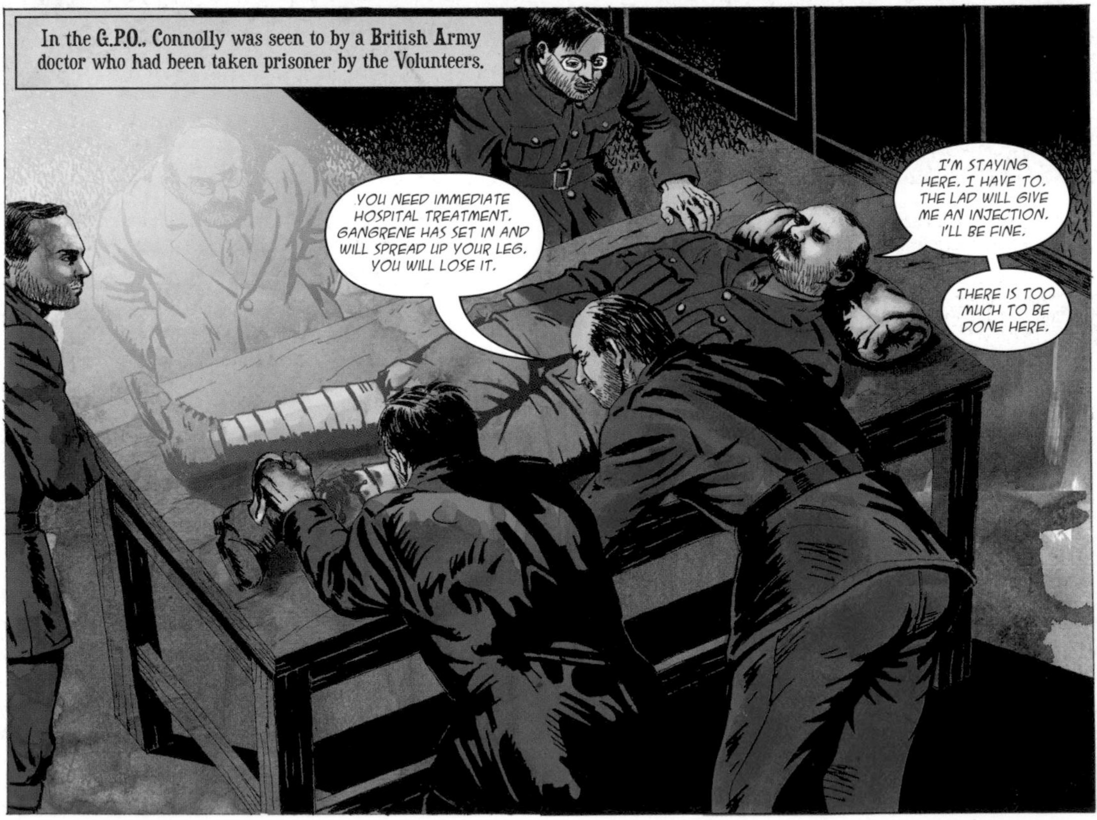
In the G.P.O., Connolly was seen to by a British Army doctor who had been taken prisoner by the Volunteers.
YOU NEED IMMEDIATE HOSPITAL TREATMENT. GANGRENE HAS SET IN AND WILL SPREAD UP YOUR LEG. YOU WILL LOSE IT.
I'M STAYING HERE. I HAVE TO. THE LAD WILL GIVE ME AN INJECTION. I'LL BE FINE.
THERE IS TOO MUCH TO BE DONE HERE.

The fighting in the South Dublin Union was continuing through the wards and corridors.

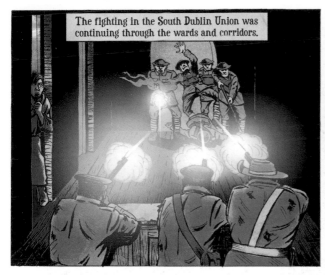

From a small yard Cathal Brugha repelled the British Troops for two hours.

Ceannt and his men, expecting an overwhelming final assault, were saying the Rosary when they heard a voice...

IT'S CATHAL BRUGHA!

GOD SAVE IRELAND, CRIED THE HERO. GOD SAVE IRELAND...

Despite his serious wounds he found the strength to sing.

...CRIED WE ALL. WHETHER THE GALLOWS HIGH OR BATTLE FIELD WE DIE...

As Ceannt approached him he was unable to stand but defiant.

WE'LL GET YOU OUT OF HERE CATHAL.

I KNOW YOU WILL BUT FIRST WE HAVE A FINAL EFFORT.

But the assault never came. Gen Lowe decided to bypass the S.D.U.

In North Earl Street Brennan-Whitmore and his men were forced to abandon the blazing buildings which they had been occupying.

WE MUST LOCATE A SAFE HOUSE WHERE WE CAN SPEND THE NIGHT.

As they entered the basement of a tenement building they were seen by a young woman from upstairs who slipped out to find some British soldiers.

As Brennan-Whitmore and his exhausted men tried to get some sleep, they were caught unawares by the tipped off British troops.

The Rebels were quickly arrested and marched to the Custom House.

As the bombardment of the G.P.O intensified Pearse decided that all the women, apart from a few nurses, should leave the building.

SIR. WE WANT TO STICK IT OUT.

WHAT HAPPENED TO EQUAL RIGHTS?

COMRADES. THIS IS NOT A REQUEST. IT'S AN ORDER.

With the building in flames Pearse insisted and the women had no option but to obey.

Plunkett and The O'Rahilly noticed their dwindling resources were being diverted.

WE'LL HAVE TO MOVE THE WOUNDED SO WE CAN FOCUS ON THE FIGHT.

AND ALSO THE PRISONERS.

Fr O'Flanagan, there to hear the rebels Easter confessions, led the wounded to Jervis Street Hospital.

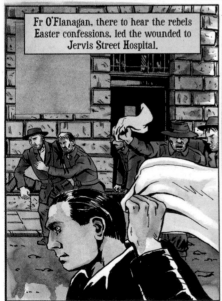

WE FIGHT TO THE LAST MAN. I WILL NOT SURRENDER. RIGHT, SEAN?

I AGREE WITH TOM. WE FIGHT ON.

YES, AGREED. BUT WE CAN NOT STAY HERE.

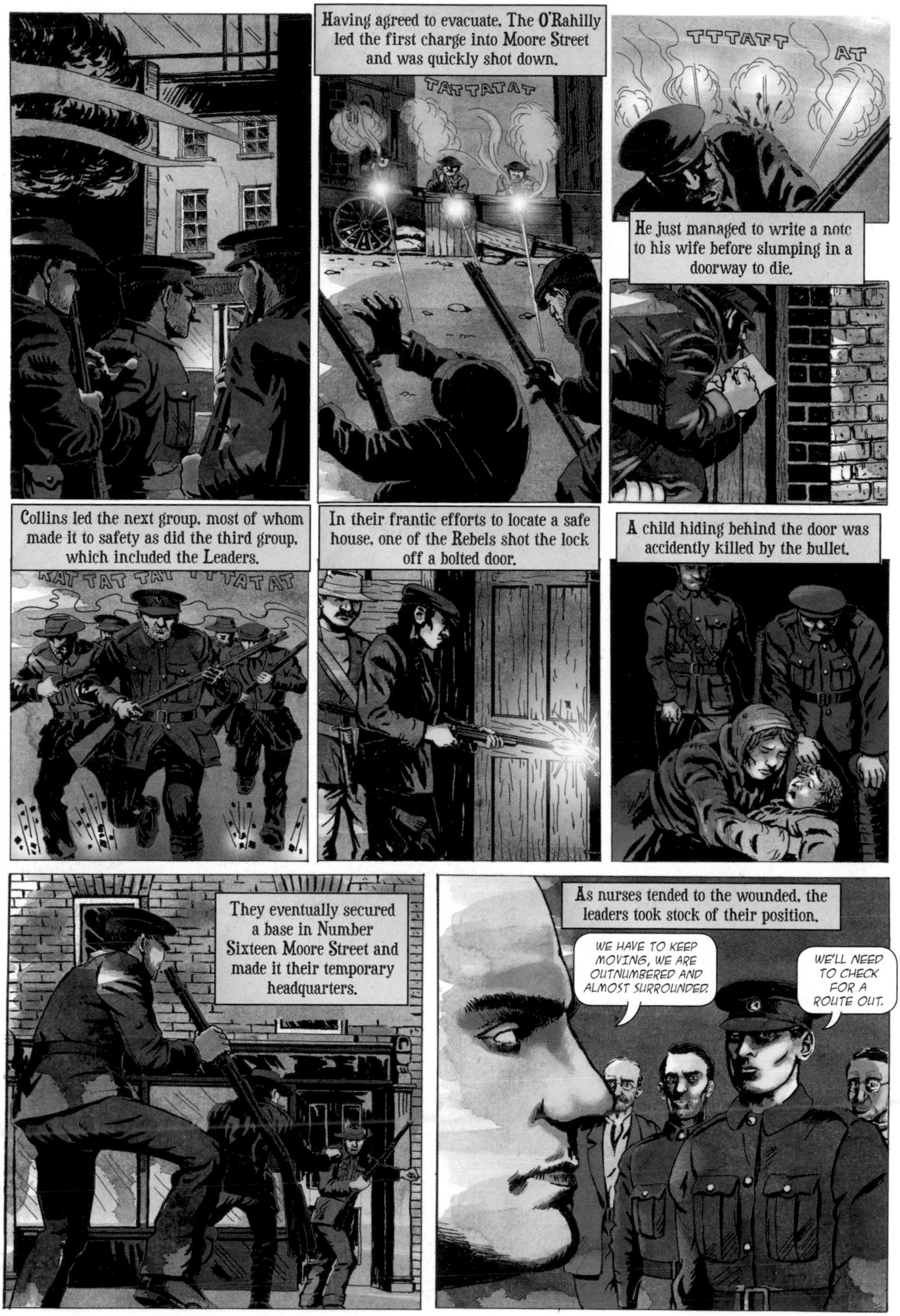

Having agreed to evacuate, The O'Rahilly led the first charge into Moore Street and was quickly shot down.
TATTATAT
TTTATT
AT
He just managed to write a note to his wife before slumping in a doorway to die.
Collins led the next group, most of whom made it to safety as did the third group, which included the Leaders.
In their frantic efforts to locate a safe house, one of the Rebels shot the lock off a bolted door.
A child hiding behind the door was accidently killed by the bullet.
They eventually secured a base in Number Sixteen Moore Street and made it their temporary headquarters.
As nurses tended to the wounded, the leaders took stock of their position.
WE HAVE TO KEEP MOVING, WE ARE OUTNUMBERED AND ALMOST SURROUNDED.
WE'LL NEED TO CHECK FOR A ROUTE OUT.

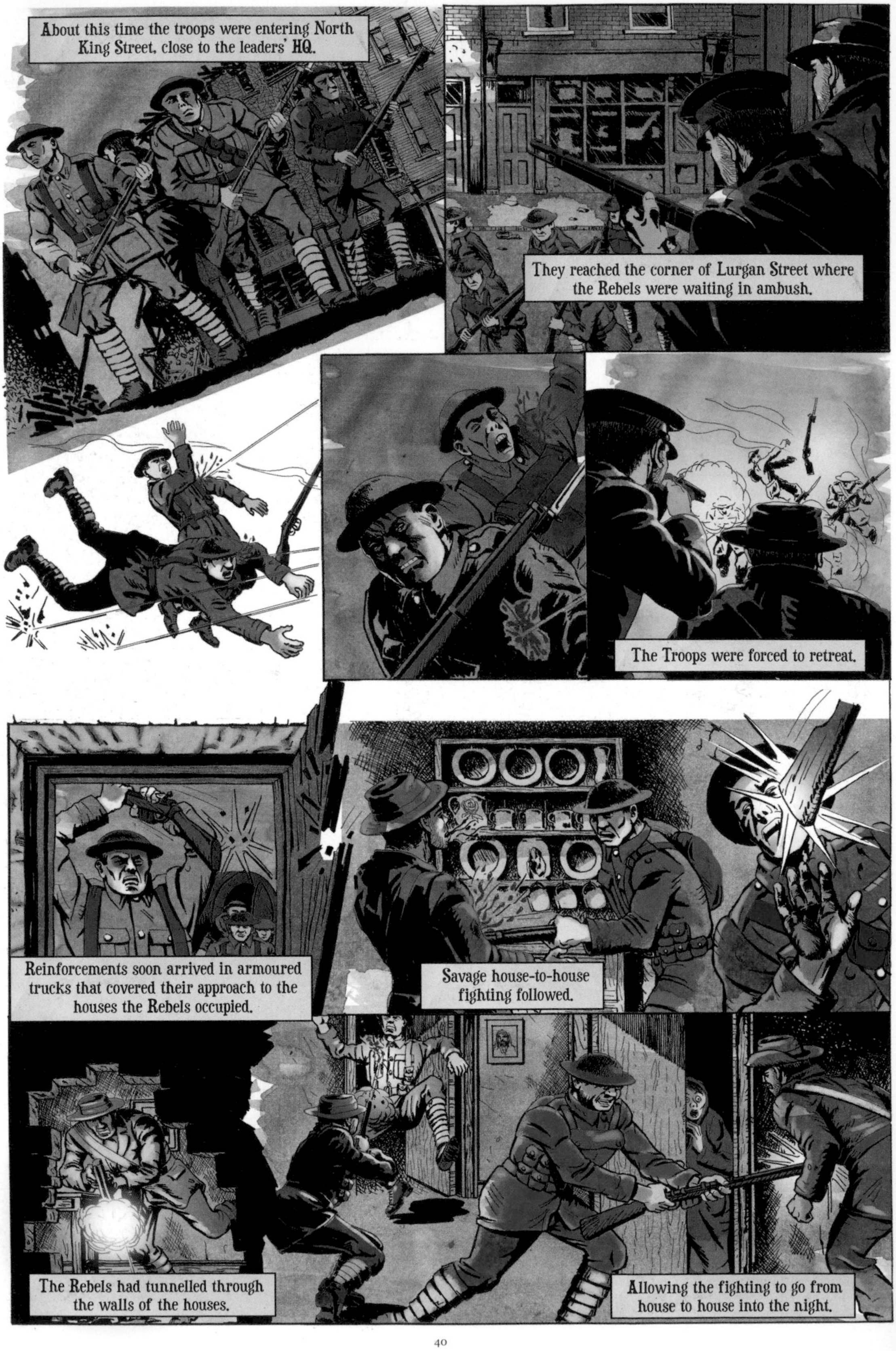
About this time the troops were entering North King Street, close to the leaders' HQ.
They reached the corner of Lurgan Street where the Rebels were waiting in ambush.
The Troops were forced to retreat.
Reinforcements soon arrived in armoured trucks that covered their approach to the houses the Rebels occupied.
Savage house-to-house fighting followed.
The Rebels had tunnelled through the walls of the houses.
Allowing the fighting to go from house to house into the night.

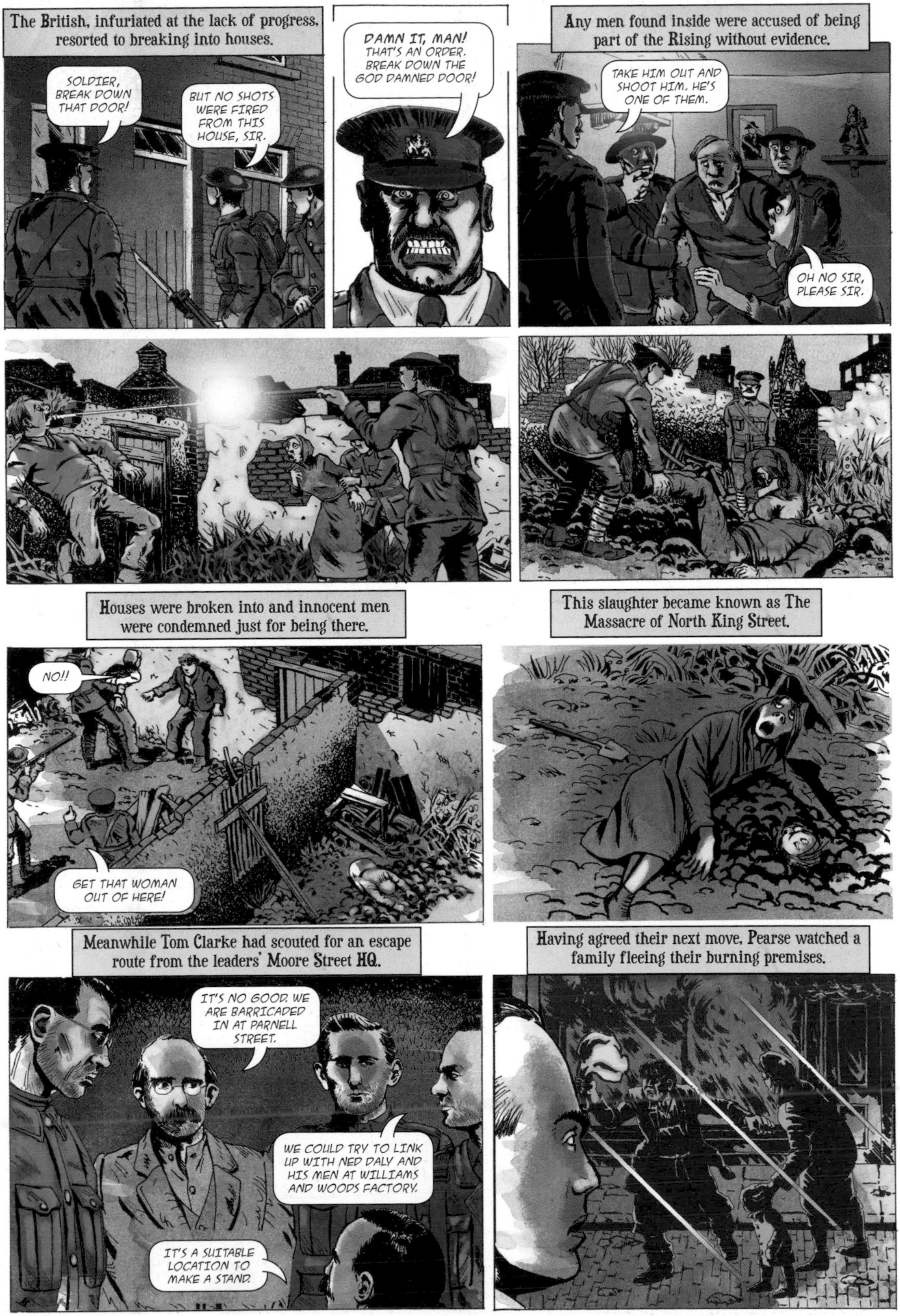

The British, infuriated at the lack of progress, resorted to breaking into houses.
SOLDIER, BREAK DOWN THAT DOOR!
BUT NO SHOTS WERE FIRED FROM THIS HOUSE, SIR.
DAMN IT, MAN! THAT'S AN ORDER. BREAK DOWN THE GOD DAMNED DOOR!
Any men found inside were accused of being part of the Rising without evidence.
TAKE HIM OUT AND SHOOT HIM. HE'S ONE OF THEM.
OH NO SIR, PLEASE SIR.
Houses were broken into and innocent men were condemned just for being there.
This slaughter became known as The Massacre of North King Street.
NO!!
GET THAT WOMAN OUT OF HERE!
Meanwhile Tom Clarke had scouted for an escape route from the leaders' Moore Street HQ.
IT'S NO GOOD. WE ARE BARRICADED IN AT PARNELL STREET.
WE COULD TRY TO LINK UP WITH NED DALY AND HIS MEN AT WILLIAMS AND WOODS FACTORY.
IT'S A SUITABLE LOCATION TO MAKE A STAND.
Having agreed their next move, Pearse watched a family fleeing their burning premises.

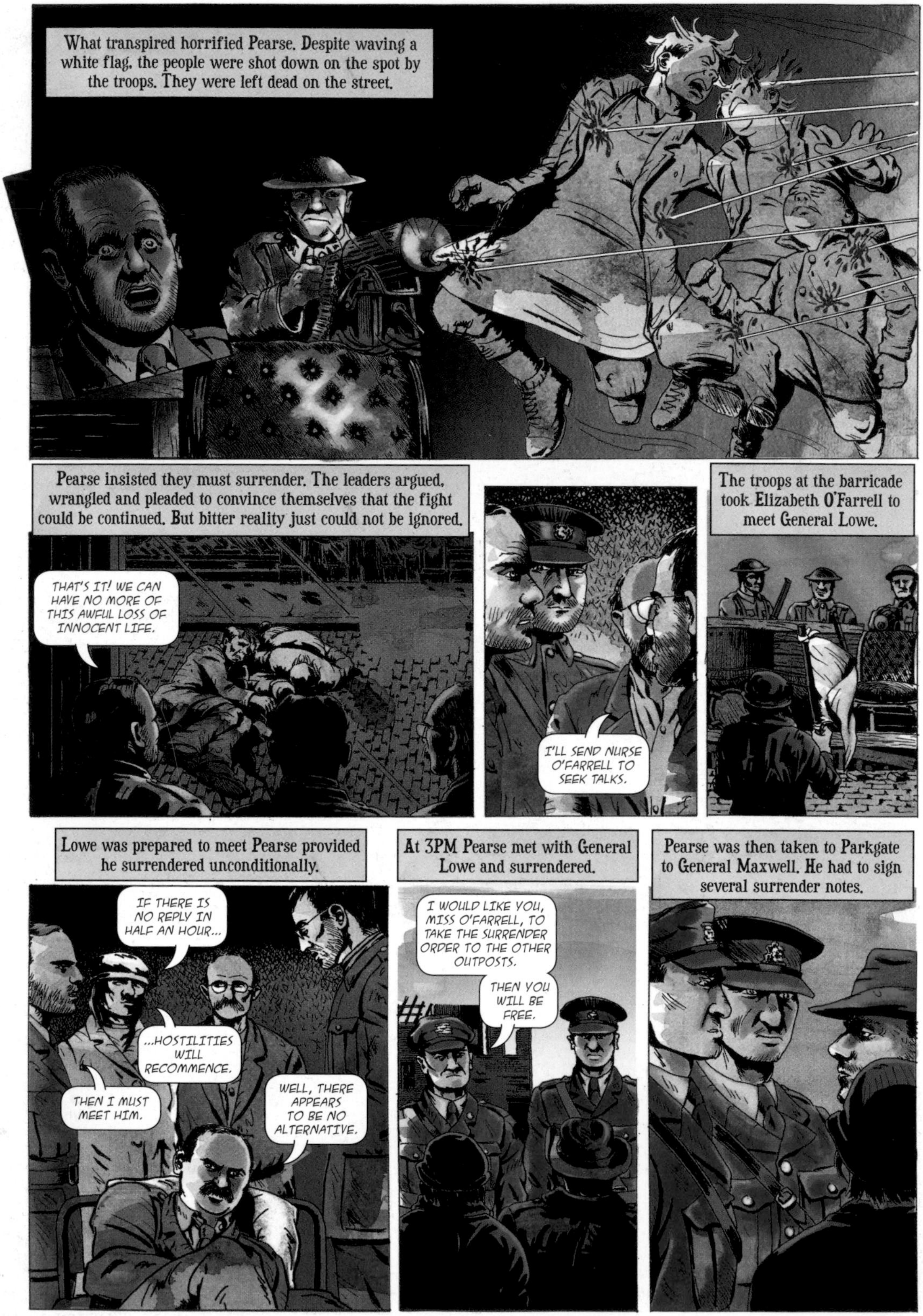
What transpired horrified Pearse. Despite waving a white flag, the people were shot down on the spot by the troops. They were left dead on the street.
Pearse insisted they must surrender. The leaders argued, wrangled and pleaded to convince themselves that the fight could be continued. But bitter reality just could not be ignored.
THAT'S IT! WE CAN HAVE NO MORE OF THIS AWFUL LOSS OF INNOCENT LIFE.
I'LL SEND NURSE O'FARRELL TO SEEK TALKS.
The troops at the barricade took Elizabeth O'Farrell to meet General Lowe.
Lowe was prepared to meet Pearse provided he surrendered unconditionally.
IF THERE IS NO REPLY IN HALF AN HOUR...
...HOSTILITIES WILL RECOMMENCE.
THEN I MUST MEET HIM.
WELL, THERE APPEARS TO BE NO ALTERNATIVE.
At 3PM Pearse met with General Lowe and surrendered.
I WOULD LIKE YOU, MISS O'FARRELL, TO TAKE THE SURRENDER ORDER TO THE OTHER OUTPOSTS.
THEN YOU WILL BE FREE.
Pearse was then taken to Parkgate to General Maxwell. He had to sign several surrender notes.

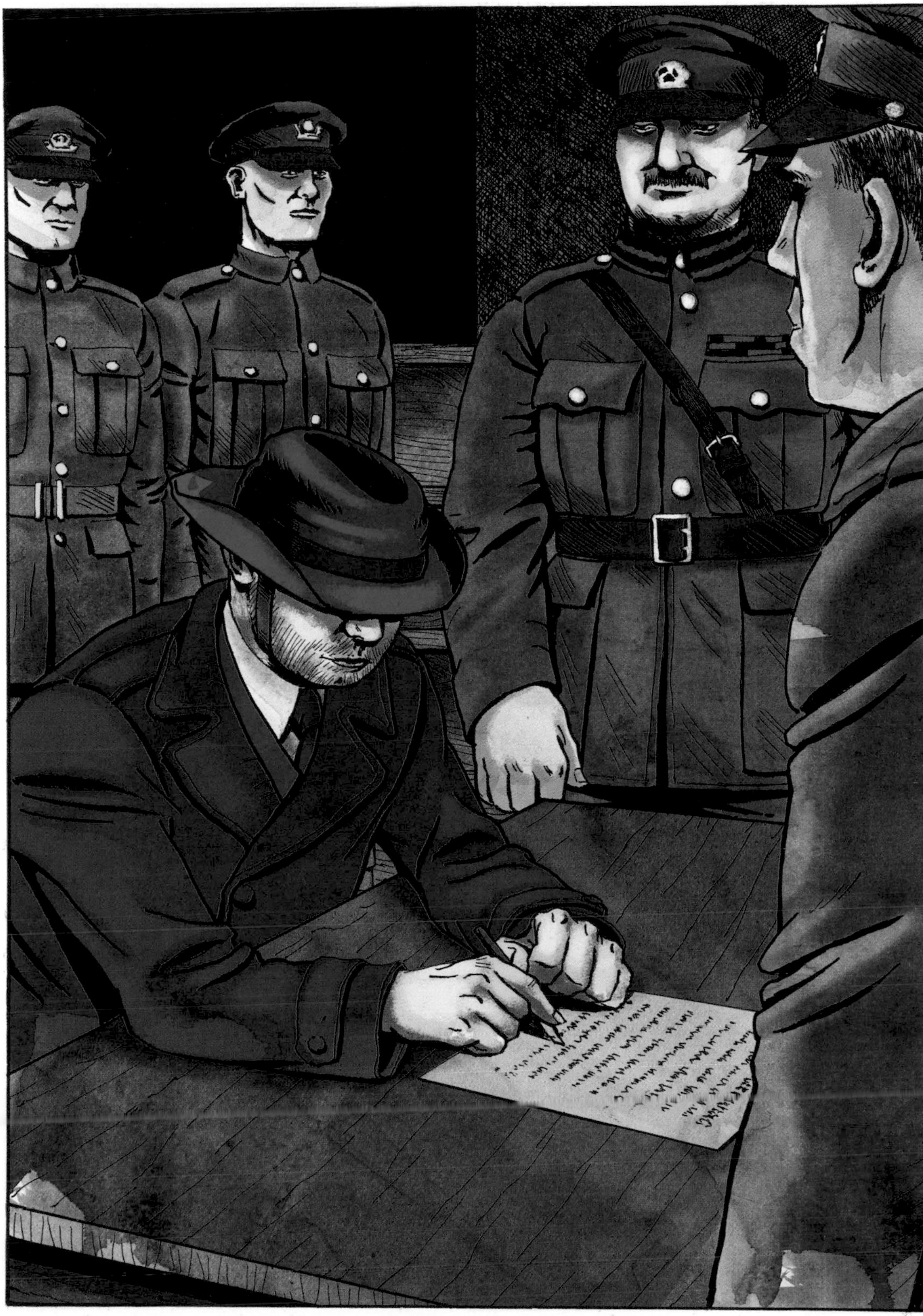

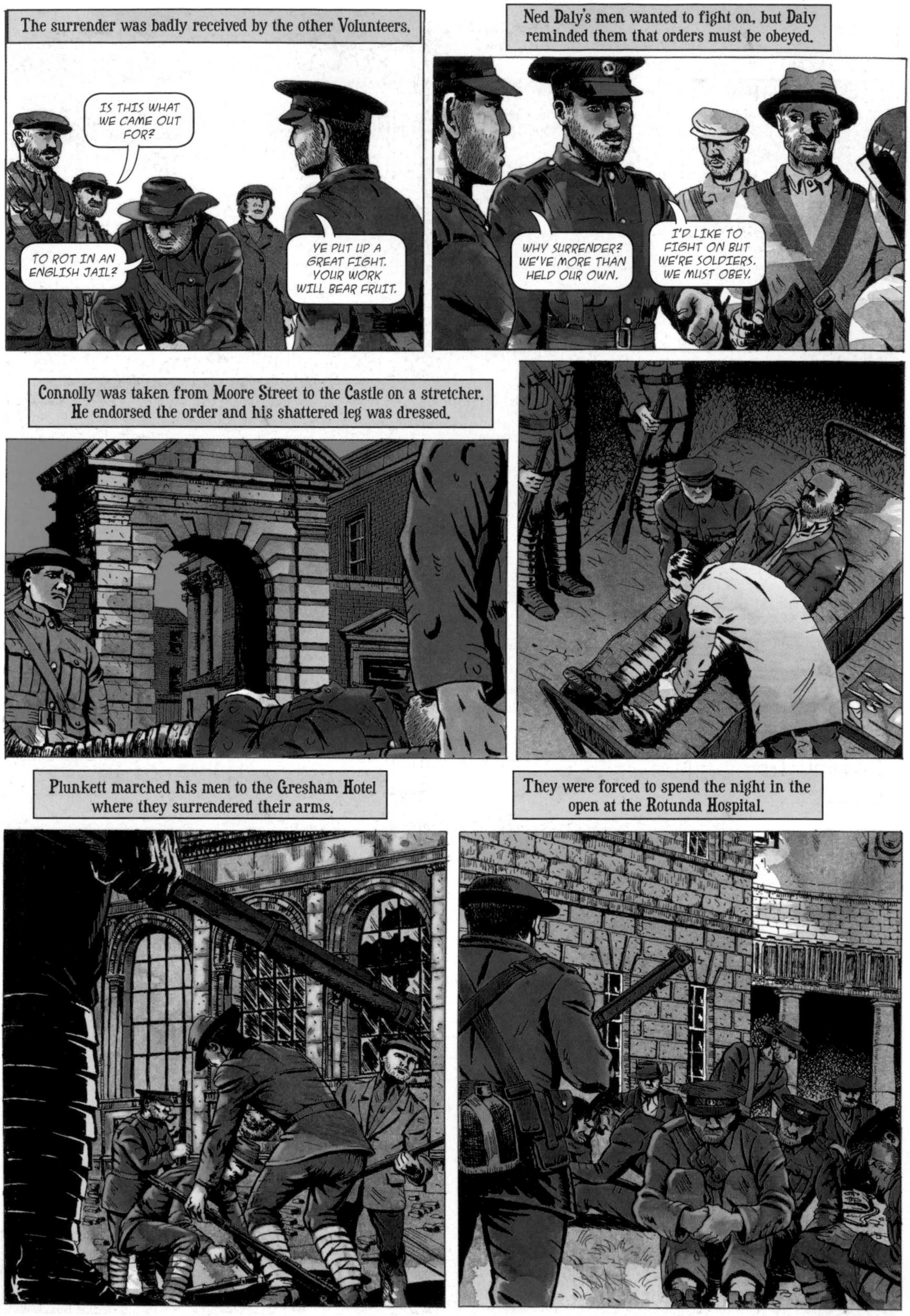
The surrender was badly received by the other Volunteers.
IS THIS WHAT WE CAME OUT FOR?
TO ROT IN AN ENGLISH JAIL?
YE PUT UP A GREAT FIGHT. YOUR WORK WILL BEAR FRUIT.
Ned Daly's men wanted to fight on, but Daly reminded them that orders must be obeyed.
WHY SURRENDER? WE'VE MORE THAN HELD OUR OWN.
I'D LIKE TO FIGHT ON BUT WE'RE SOLDIERS. WE MUST OBEY.
Connolly was taken from Moore Street to the Castle on a stretcher. He endorsed the order and his shattered leg was dressed.
Plunkett marched his men to the Gresham Hotel where they surrendered their arms.
They were forced to spend the night in the open at the Rotunda Hospital.

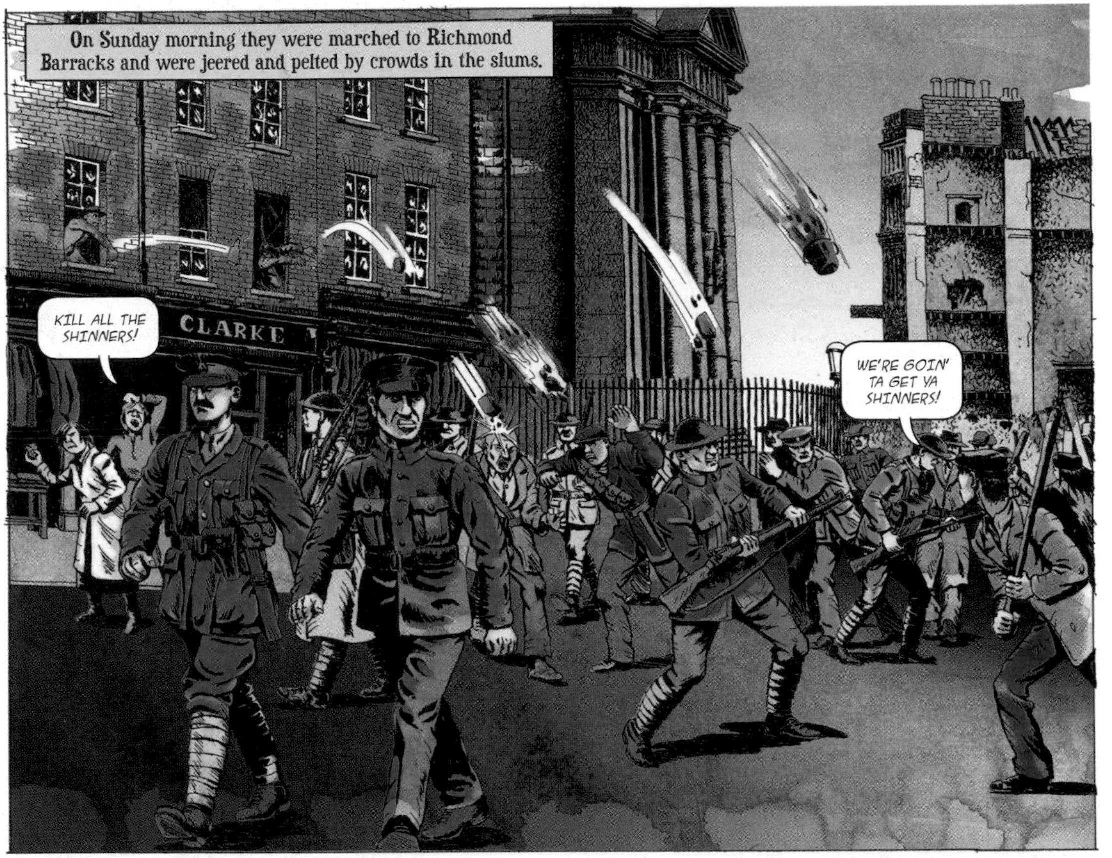
On Sunday morning they were marched to Richmond Barracks and were jeered and pelted by crowds in the slums.
KILL ALL THE SHINNERS!
CLARKE
WE'RE GOIN' TA GET YA SHINNERS!

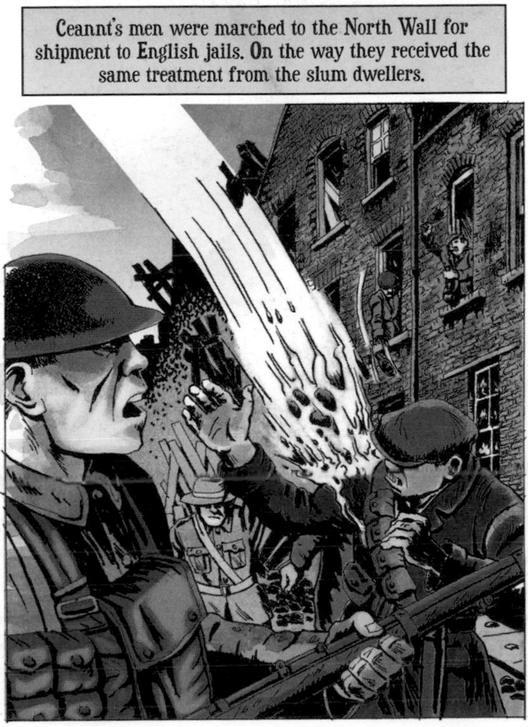
Ceannt's men were marched to the North Wall for shipment to English jails. On the way they received the same treatment from the slum dwellers.

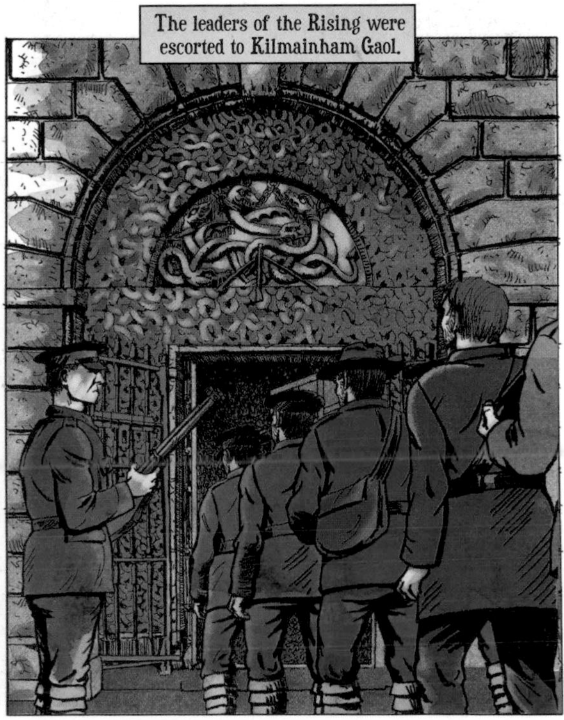
The leaders of the Rising were escorted to Kilmainham Gaol.

Thursday 4th May 1916, 2AM

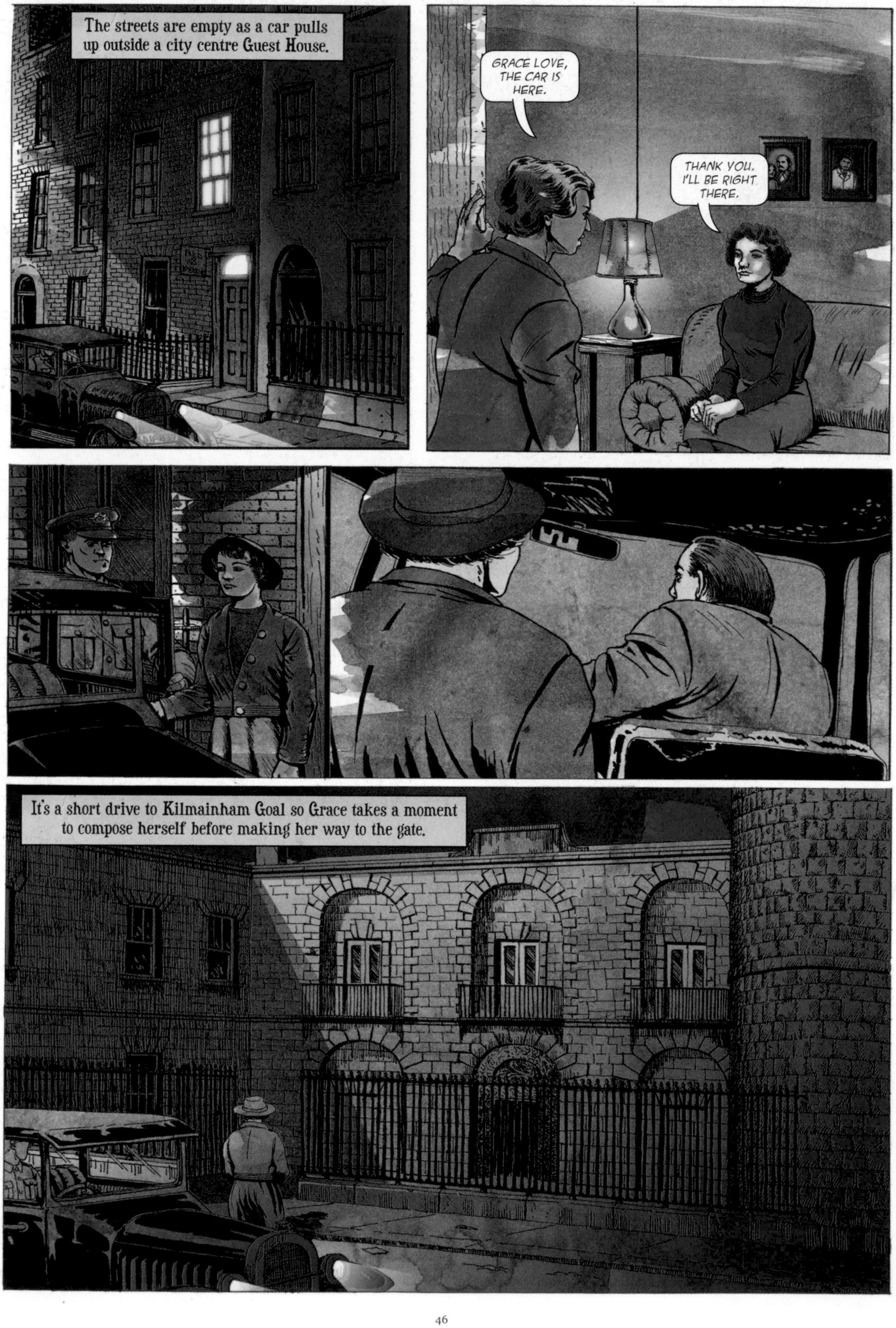
The streets are empty as a car pulls up outside a city centre Guest House.
GRACE LOVE, THE CAR IS HERE.
THANK YOU. I'LL BE RIGHT THERE.
It's a short drive to Kilmainham Goal so Grace takes a moment to compose herself before making her way to the gate.

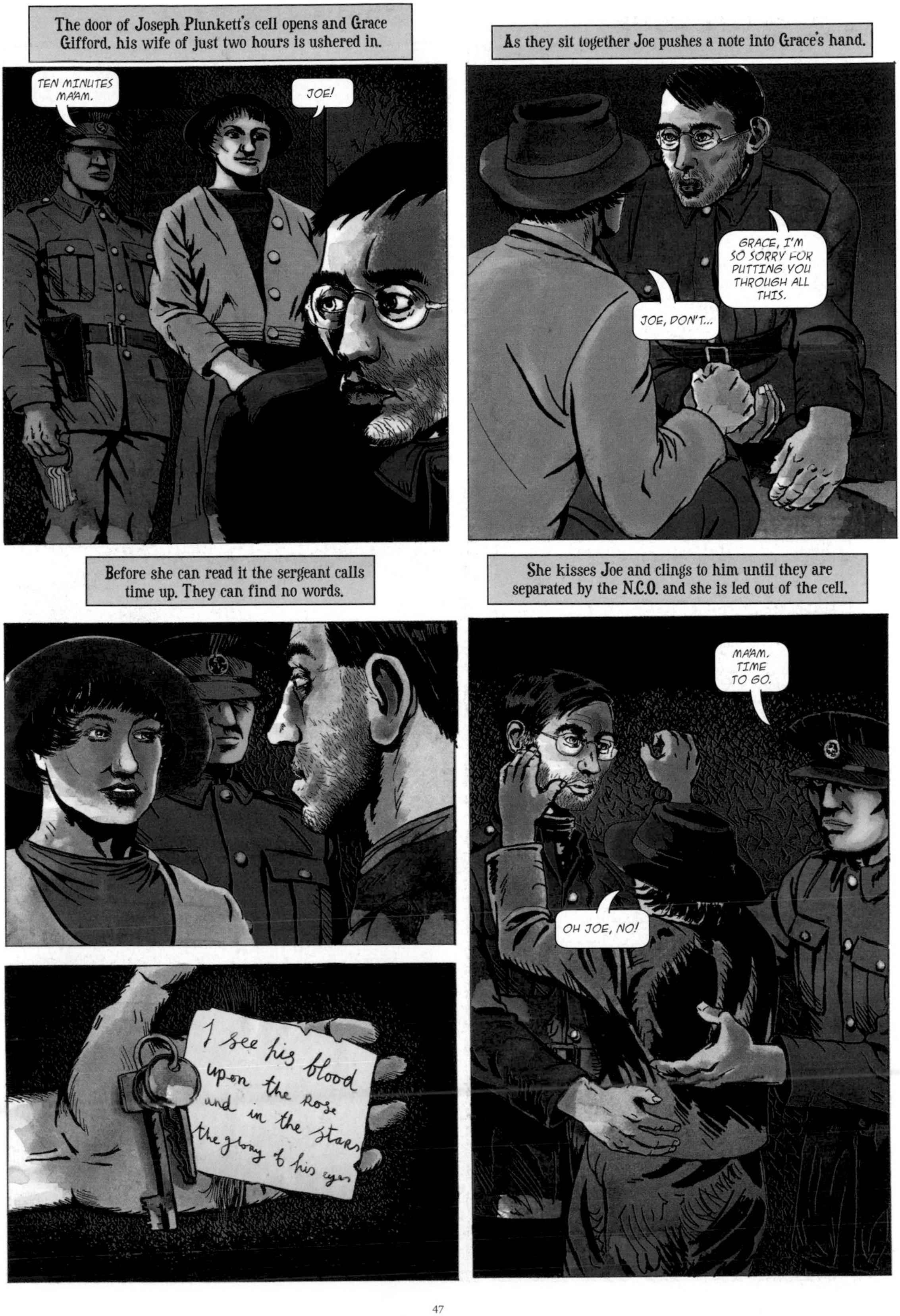
The door of Joseph Plunkett's cell opens and Grace Gifford, his wife of just two hours is ushered in.
TEN MINUTES MA'AM.
JOE!
As they sit together Joe pushes a note into Grace's hand.
GRACE, I'M SO SORRY FOR PUTTING YOU THROUGH ALL THIS.
JOE, DON'T...
Before she can read it the sergeant calls time up. They can find no words.
I see his blood upon the rose and in the stars the glory of his eyes
She kisses Joe and clings to him until they are separated by the N.C.O. and she is led out of the cell.
MA'AM. TIME TO GO.
OH JOE, NO!

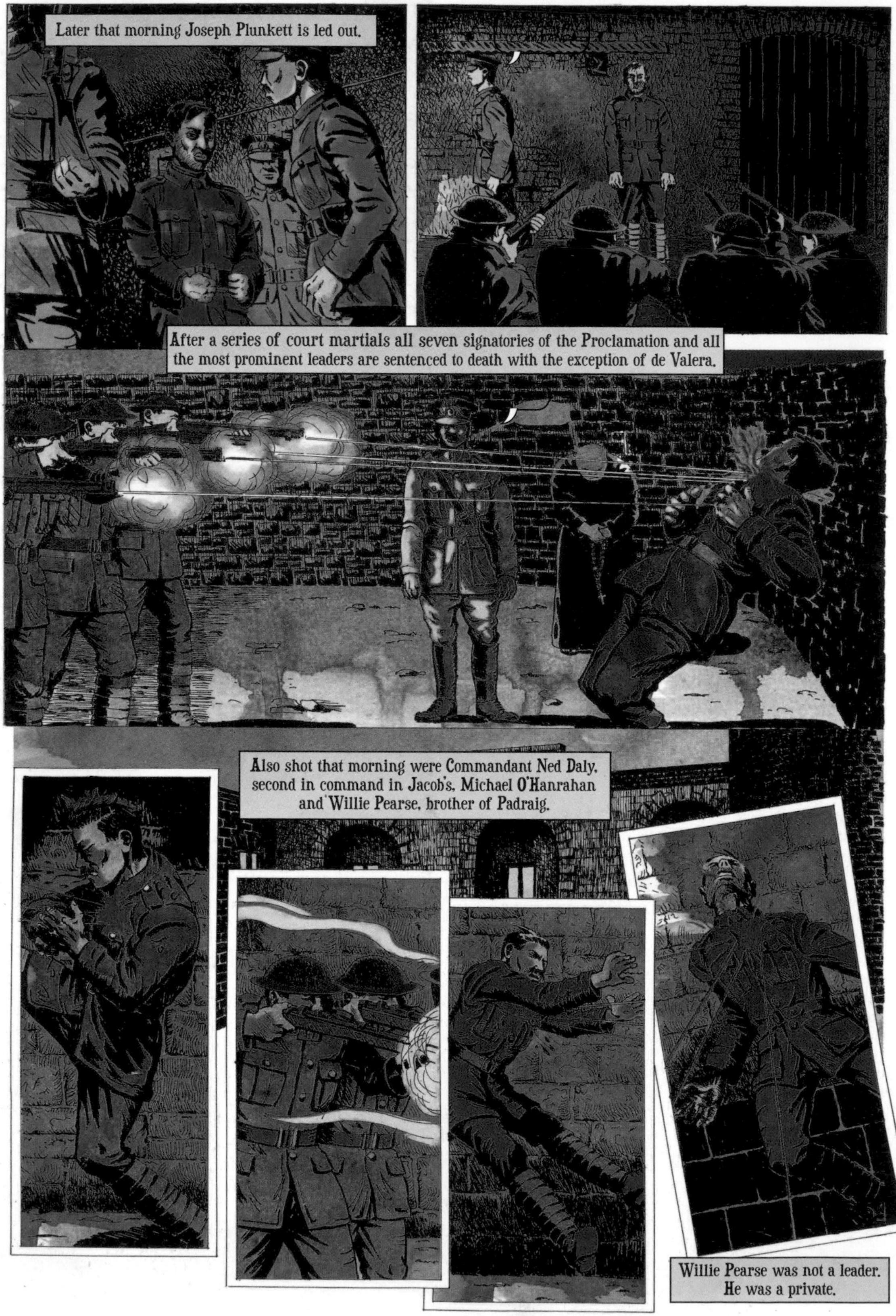

Later that morning Joseph Plunkett is led out.
After a series of court martials all seven signatories of the Proclamation and all the most prominent leaders are sentenced to death with the exception of de Valera.
Also shot that morning were Commandant Ned Daly, second in command in Jacob's, Michael O'Hanrahan and Willie Pearse, brother of Padraig.
Willie Pearse was not a leader. He was a private.